MATTHIAS LOY

The Doctrine of Justification

Contents

PREFACE TO THE SECOND EDITION.   v

PREFACE TO THE FIRST EDITION.   vi

Introduction   viii

The Nature of Justification   1

    Section I.   2

JUSTIFICATION NOT A DECLARATION DEFINING
THE SINNER'S MORAL CONDITION.   2

    Section 2.   5

JUSTIFICATION IS NOT A DIVINE ACT MAKING
THE SINNER JUST   5

    Section 3.   14

JUSTIFICATION IS A DIVINE DECLARATION
CHANGING THE SINNER'S RELATION TO GOD.   14

The Ground of Justification   21

    Section I.   22

THE GROUND OF JUSTIFICATION IS NOT MAN'S
NATURAL WORTHINESS.   23

    Section 2.   27

THE GROUND OF JUSTIFICATION IS NOT ANY
HUMAN ACQUIREMENT.   27

    Section 3.   31

THE GROUND OF JUSTIFICATION IS THE GRACE
OF GOD AND THE MERITS OF CHRIST.   31

The Means of Its Bestowal   40

    Section I.   40

JUSTIFICATION REQUIRES MEANS TO BESTOW IT.   41

    Section 2.   46

THE WORD OF GOD   46

Section 3.   55

THE HOLY SACRAMENTS.   55

Section 4.   63

THE DIVINE BESTOWAL IS NOT THE HUMAN
POSSESSION.   63

The Means of Its Reception   68

Section 1.   68

NO MEANS OF RECEPTION BESIDES FAITH.   69

Section 2.   71

FAITH IS THE DESIGNATED MEANS OF RECEP-
TION.   71

Section 3.   78

NO CONDITION TO BE FULFILLED BEFORE FAITH
AVAILS.   78

Section 4.   81

THE NATURE OF JUSTIFYING FAITH.   81

Section 5.   89

HOW FAITH JUSTIFIES.   89

Section 6.   94

DEGREES IN FAITH, BUT NOT IN JUSTIFICATION.   95

Its Effects   105

Section I.   106

IT GIVES THE CONSCIENCE PEACE.   106

Section 2.   112

IT SECURES SANCTIFICATION.   112

Section 3.   116

IT RENDERS GLORY TO GOD.   116

CONCLUSION.   119

PREFACE TO THE SECOND EDITION.

THE first edition of the book which is here for a second time offered to the public was all sold within a few years after its publication in 1869. Since then the author has frequently been solicited to prepare a new edition. Having been assured that the unpretending volume has done some service in the cause of saving truth, and that there is still sufficient demand for it to encourage the hope of further salutary fruits, he has finally consented to its republication. He hopes that the few changes and the additions which he has made, will render the work somewhat more worthy of the patronage which it has received and increase the usefulness at which it aims. May God continue to bless the little volume in its new and improved form, and render it instrumental in promoting the glory of His great name and the welfare of precious souls.

Columbus, October, 1881.

PREFACE TO THE FIRST EDITION.

THE celebration of the Seventh Jubilee of the Reformation has directed the thoughts of many Protestants anew to the old paths in which our fathers walked, and to the old treasures in which their hearts rejoiced. Those paths, which had been by many traditionally regarded as crooked and rugged, are found, upon a closer view, to be delightfully straight and smooth; and those treasures, which have so often been decried as rough and rusty, are seen, upon a more careful inspection, to be pure and precious.

The children are learning to love again what those noble heroes of other days deemed passing lovely.

Among the old treasures of the Church the pure doctrine of Justification by Faith holds a conspicuous place. It is a pearl, with which not all the wealth of the world could have induced the men of the Reformation to part. It is a garland of rarest flowers, whose beauty and fragrance afforded them ever new delight. It is a citadel, within which they felt themselves secure against every foe, and for which they fought with a vigor and a valor that challenges the admiration of all time. The Church could not live and flourish without it. She grows weak when she neglects it; she is strong when she holds it to her heart. It is the criterion of her condition.

When the thoughts of Christians are turned towards the stirring times of the Reformation, this cardinal doctrine must necessarily claim a large share of attention. It is true, since the days of Luther it has always been confessed by the Church which bears his honored name, and this confession has been echoed by other Protestants all over the world. And yet a renewed study of the subject seems to us to be a want of the times. Doctrines and practices have come into vogue which are not in harmony with it, and which a clearer apprehension of it would tend to banish from the Church. The Pelagian poison of Romanism is infecting many who are most ready to denounce Rome; and the only effectual antidote is the blessed Gospel of the grace of God, with its cheering proclamation of the sinner's justification through faith alone, without the deeds of the law. Only where this doctrine is" understood and embraced is the Gospel pure and plain and precious.

We do not expect to contribute anything materially new on this delightful theme. The truth is old, and our aim is to present and illustrate this old truth as the Bible contains it and the Church of the Reformation confesses it. If we could render it clearer to the minds and dearer to the hearts of some who sigh for the Consolation of Israel, our ambition would be fully satisfied and our labor richly compensated. To this end may God bless our humble essay.

Introduction

WHEN, in answer to the troubled question, "What must I do to be saved?" the inspired preachers of the everlasting Gospel said, "Believe on the Lord Jesus Christ, and thou shalt be saved," a way of deliverance from sin and death was shown, of which Nature gives no information. The question is one which has occupied the thoughts of earnest men in all ages of the world. Since sin has entered into the world, and death by sin, human hearts have trembled at the doom which was felt to be impending, and human reason has been unable to find a way of escape. "We speak the wisdom of God in a mystery, even the hidden wisdom which God ordained before the world unto our glory; which none of the princes of this world knew." (1 Cor, 2:7, 8.) They groped in darkness after "the unknown God," and blindly sought, in impossible ways, deliverance from the burden of sin. Natural religion furnishes no ground of hope, and brings to the troubled conscience no words of peace. The Gospel alone supplies the want of groaning humanity and offers the remedy for its deadly spiritual disease; and of this Gospel the sum and substance is justification by faith through Jesus' blood. "I am not ashamed of the Gospel of Christ: for it is the power of God unto salvation to everyone that believeth; to the Jew first, and also to the Greek. For therein is the righteousness of God revealed from faith to faith: as it is written, The just shall live by faith." (Rom. 1:16, 17.) "All things are of God, who hath reconciled us to Himself by Jesus Christ, and hath given to us the ministry of reconciliation; to wit, that God was in Christ, reconciling the world unto Himself, not imputing their trespasses unto them; and hath committed unto us the Word of reconciliation. Now then we are ambassadors for Christ, as though God did beseech you by us: we pray you in Christ's stead, be ye reconciled to God. For He hath made Him to be sin for us, Who knew no sin;

that we might be made the righteousness of God in Him." (2 Cor. 5:18-21.)

This great doctrine of the sinner's justification by faith in the Redeemer of the world, who lived and suffered and died to save our lost race, is the very soul of the supernatural revelation given in Holy Scripture. But it is, therefore, also the doctrine against which the attacks of Satan are mainly directed, and against which the world and the flesh most obstinately array themselves. "After that in the wisdom of God the world by wisdom knew not God, it pleased God by the foolishness of preaching to save them that believe. For the Jews require a sign, and the Greeks seek after wisdom: but we preach Christ crucified — unto the Jews a stumbling-block, and unto the Greeks foolishness; but unto them which are called, both Jews and Greeks, Christ the power of God, and the wisdom of God." (2 Cor. 1:21-24.) Satan in his malice hates the Savior, as he hates the salvation of man, whose ruin he has compassed; and man in his pride despises the gracious plan which divine wisdom has formed for his deliverance, because that plan gives no credit to his genius for devising nor to his power for executing it. Human reason and human inclination are therefore always, in their natural state, averse to the doctrine of Justification by faith. Hence it is no wonder that earth and hell combine in persistent efforts to banish it from the Church and from the world.

It was this doctrine that formed the center of the whole controversy in the glorious Reformation of the sixteenth century, and upon the maintenance of which Luther's whole work depended. Both in regard to doctrine and to life it forms the sum of the whole evangelical system. Therefore the Evangelical Church, in opposition to the naturalistic corruptions of Rome, declares in the Apology of the Augsburg Confession: "Since this controversy concerns the principal and most important article of the whole Christian doctrine, so that very much depends upon this article, which also chiefly serves to a clear, correct understanding of the entire Holy Scriptures, and alone shows the way to the unspeakable treasure and the true knowledge of Christ; yea, which is the only key to the whole Bible, and without which the poor conscience can have no true, constant, certain hope, nor understand the riches of Christ's grace: — we pray your Imperial Majesty graciously to hear us, as the case requires, concerning these great, grave, and all-important matters. For as our adversaries do not understand or know what is meant in the Scriptures by forgiveness of sins, by faith, by grace, by righteousness, they have miserably defiled this noble, indispensable, and principal article, without which no one can know Christ; they have entirely suppressed the exalted, precious treasure of the knowledge of Christ, or of what Christ and what His kingdom and grace are, and have wretchedly robbed poor consciences of this great and noble treasure and everlasting consolation, upon which everything depends." (Art. iv. 2, 3.) Furthermore, in the Smalcald Articles the Church declares in reference to "the chief article" of Justification: "Whatever may happen, though heaven and earth should fall, nothing in this article can be yielded or rescinded. 'For there is none other name under heaven given among men whereby we must be saved,' says St. Peter (Art iv. 12); 'and with His stripes we are healed.' (Art. liii. 5.) Upon this article rests all that we teach and do against the pope, the devil, and all the world. We must therefore be entirely certain of this, and not doubt it; otherwise all will be lost, and the pope and the devil and all that opposes, will prevail and obtain the victory." (Part II., Art. i.)

Luther in many places gives expression to his deep conviction and intense appreciation of the importance which attaches to this cardinal doctrine. With him, as with all the children of God who have found peace in believing, it was not a beautiful speculative theory, but a question of the everlasting salvation of millions of perishing souls. Dying men are justified by faith, or they are not justified at all. They are saved through Christ, or they perish forever. If this doctrine of Justification is abandoned, all is lost; with it Christianity falls, and the world goes down in everlasting woe. It is the article with which the Church stands or falls. Commenting on Genesis 21:17, Luther says of Justification: "This is the principal article of our faith. If this be set aside, as is done by the Jews, or be corrupted, as is done by the papists, the Church cannot continue, neither can the glory of God be maintained, which consists in this, that He is merciful, and that for the sake of His Son He forgives sins and bestows salvation." (Erl. Lat., v. 137.) Again, he says on Galatians 2:11: "As I have before said, Paul has here in hand no indifferent trifle, but the highest article of all Christian doctrine. To him who rightly understands the utility and majesty of this article all other things will seem vile and worthless. For in comparison with this article of Justification, what are Peter and Paul, what are an angel from heaven or all creatures? If we know this, we have the clearest light: if we are ignorant of it, we are in the densest darkness. Wherefore, if you see this article impugned or defaced, fear not to resist either St. Peter or an angel from heaven; for it cannot be sufficiently magnified and extolled." (Jb. 1:159.)

In his Commentary on John 6:53, he says of Justification by faith: "Where this article remains in our pulpits there is no danger: we are safe against heretics and errors. This article suffers no error to be associated with it; the Holy Ghost is also present where it is, and those who believe it tolerate no error. If they are led astray, it is a sure sign that they did not understand this article: if they had rightly apprehended it, they would not have been deceived. All other doctrines, even if the words are spoken which we use, are of nothing but good works; as our factious spirits, when examined in the light, teach only of good works, and do not understand that life, grace, and salvation come without our work through faith." (Erl., xlviii. 18.)

This cardinal doctrine, whose importance cannot be over-estimated, the Lutheran Church has always joyfully confessed and patiently taught, to the glory of the Redeemer and the welfare of the redeemed. And there is need that this should be continued. Many are slow to learn it, and those who zealously study it and meditate upon it find that its marvelous wisdom is not so easily mastered. It is no indication of thorough acquaintance with the doctrine, in all its import and bearings, to speak of it as a simple lesson for children merely. Children may learn it, and be happy in its sunshine; but mature minds may study it with ever-increasing light. Luther apprehended the doctrine with a clearness and preached it with a power that had no equal since the days of St. Paul; and yet he says: "When you hear an unripe saint boasting that he knows quite well we must be saved by grace, without works, and pretending that this is for him an easy art, you may be sure that he knows not whereof he affirms, and perhaps will never experience it. For it is not an art which can be perfectly mastered, or which we can boast of having learned:

it is an art that insists on being master, and requires us to remain pupils. And those who rightly understand it do not boast that they know all about it; but they perceive something of it, as a pleasant odor, which they eagerly pursue, which they wonder at, but which they cannot comprehend or fully possess as they desire; they hunger and thirst and pant for it, with ever-increasing longing, and can never get enough of hearing and handling it, — as St. Paul himself confesses that he had not yet attained it, and Christ pronounces those blessed who hunger and thirst after righteousness — Mat. v." (Erl., xl. 325.)

Let us not, then, suppose that the old theme contains nothing to which we could yet profitably give earnest attention. Many, it is to be feared, have not yet so far entered its beautiful garden as to experience its delights. To them it will be a blessing to enter and behold the wonders which God hath wrought, and taste that He is gracious. Those who have had a taste of these heavenly sweets will be glad of any contribution, however small, to the stock of that knowledge which is their daily strength and comfort and joy. May the Holy Spirit lead us into all truth as it is in Jesus our Righteousness, and by the truth make us free!

Justification is the gracious act of God by which He declares the sinner righteous, removing the sentence of condemnation and imputing to him a perfect holiness. The cause of this declaration cannot be the sinner's worthiness; for then he would not be a sinner. We can find the ground of God's act only in His abounding grace, which seeks the welfare of men, even though they have, by their iniquity, forfeited all claims upon the divine blessing, and in the merits of Jesus, whom that grace has sent into the world to atone for human sin. Our participation in the benefits of this atonement does not grow out of our inheritance of human nature; for that would involve the actual salvation of all men, in direct contradiction to the Scriptures: nor are we justified by a divine act which takes place in the distant realms of heaven without reaching the souls of men, whose salvation it is designed to secure; for that would exclude the necessity, so often urged in the Scriptures, of repentance and of faith in the Gospel. There must be a medium of communicating with the sinner, and the Bible points us to the means of grace as God's merciful institution to effect such communication.

But the conveyance of grace, and the publication of a cheering declaration, would be of no avail to us unless we appropriated them as our own; and such appropriation can, according to the Scriptures, be made only by faith. The believer does not stand in doubting expectation of some miraculous occurrence by which he shall know himself justified; but he appropriates the merits of Christ in all their fullness, and thus has peace in believing, is thoroughly furnished unto all good works, in which he abounds to the glory of God, and knows himself to be an heir of Heaven through Christ. Such a joyful child of God earnestly guards against every form of error that would tarnish the purity of the precious doctrine of Justification.

These propositions we propose in the following essay to elucidate. We shall, accordingly, in presenting the great Doctrine of Justification, treat of: I. Its Nature; II. Its Ground; III. The Means of its Bestowal; IV. The Means of its Appropriation; and V. Its Effects.

1

The Nature of Justification

HOW shall man, the miserable sinner and child of wrath by nature, be justified before his God? He cannot justify himself: his iniquity is inexcusable, his damnation is just. Yet the Scriptures not only speak of a justification, but make it the very heart of the Christian revelation. Without it not a soul could be saved from the eternal death which is the sinner's due and doom. Man cannot justify himself before God; but it does not follow that justification is impossible. "It is God that justifieth." He declares "at this time His righteousness: that He might be just, and the justifier of him that believeth in Jesus." (Rom. 3:26.) Wherein this divine act consists it behooves us all to understand.

Justification may be conceived as a declaration of God by which the sinner's moral condition is designated. Or, it may be thought an exercise of divine power by which an intrinsic change is wrought in the sinner. Or, finally, it may be considered a divine declaration by which the transgressor is brought into a new relation to his God. A glance at each of these propositions will suffice to secure the conviction that there is a material divergence in the views which they express. An examination of the Scriptures will make it manifest that the last alone contains the Biblical truth concerning the nature of Justification, while the other two, though popular, are pernicious forms of error.

Section I.

JUSTIFICATION NOT A DECLARATION DEFINING THE SINNER'S MORAL CONDITION.

St. Paul declares (Rom. 3:23-25): "All have sinned and come short of the glory of God; being justified freely by His grace through the redemption that is in Christ Jesus: whom God hath set forth to be a propitiation through faith in His blood, to declare His righteousness for the remission of sins that are past, through the forbearance of God."

From this it is evident, in the first place, that the person to be justified is a sinner. Any declaration, therefore, which is designed to indicate his true moral condition, must imply his sinfulness. No other could be in harmony with the fact. God could not, if the purpose were to give a correct representation of the sinner's actual state, pronounce him just; for this would be simply asserting that he is not a sinner, and thus directly contradicting the plain truth.

In the Epistle to the Romans, in which the doctrine of Justification by faith is expressly and fully set forth and explained, St. Paul begins his exposition by showing that the whole world is under condemnation because of sin, and that, therefore, there can be no salvation except in Christ. Jews and Gentiles alike are represented as having departed from God and become utterly corrupt. "There is no difference; for all have sinned and come short of the glory of God." (Rom. 3:22, 23.) There is not a just person among the children of men. "The whole world lieth in wickedness." (2 John 19.) It is the poor publican who smites upon his breast and prays, "God be merciful to me a sinner," that is justified; not the proud Pharisee who thanks God that he is not sinful like other people. The righteousness of God by faith presupposes the unrighteousness of man, to whom it is to be imputed. It is the unjust person that is justified by the grace of God in Christ Jesus our Lord. "The Scripture hath concluded ail under sin, that the promise by faith of Jesus Christ might be given to them that believe." (Gal. 3:22.)

Hence it is clear that justification is not the expression of a divine judgment in reference to the moral condition of its object. This could be no justification at all; because the person to whom the judgment refers, is unjust in fact, and could not, without a gross violation of truth, be pronounced, with reference to his moral state, otherwise than unjust.

Secondly, such a view of justification, is in conflict with the statement that this act of God takes place freely, by His grace, and through His forbearance. For it requires no condescending mercy to predicate of man what is justly his due. If he were just, it would be no manifestation of grace to declare him just. If he were not a sinner, there would be no divine forbearance needed to refrain from pronouncing sentence of condemnation upon him. If he were righteous, there would be a moral necessity for recognizing him as such, and no propriety in the use of the word "freely" in connection with such recognition. That we are justified "freely" implies that there is nothing in us which could furnish God a motive for declaring us just. That we are justified "by His grace" implies that the cause is in God alone, who pities us in our lost estate. That we are justified "through the forbearance of God" implies that there is abundant reason to condemn us, but that divine mercy triumphs over justice in setting the sinner free. It would be trampling upon the words of Scripture to assume that justification is an act which merely gives man his due. That which is due to him is eternal damnation. "The wages of sin is death; but the gift of God is eternal life through Jesus Christ our Lord." (Rom. 6:23.) When a sinner is justified, he receives what is not his due: he is unjust, but is declared just, freely, by the grace of God.

Thirdly, the righteousness, in view of which the sinner is declared just, is represented as one which is not inherent in him and does not belong to his moral condition. For it is asserted to be the righteousness of God — a righteousness which God alone bestows, and which alone avails before Him. And, to guard against any misunderstanding, it is further affirmed that this righteousness is "without the law" (Rom. 3:21), and that "by the deeds of the law there shall no flesh be justified in His sight." (lb. 20.) If man's moral condition were righteous, he might, indeed, be pronounced righteous, — but not in view of "the righteousness of God, which is by faith of Jesus Christ" (3:22), and not "without the deeds of the law." The law requires him to be righteous; but he has failed to comply with the requirement: therefore God justifies him freely, by His grace, on the ground of a righteousness which belongs to another. Justification would be by the righteousness of man, not by the righteousness of God, and by the deeds of the law, wherein such human righteousness consists, if it were merely a declaration attributing to man what he really possesses. But by the law is the knowledge of sin. It does not secure the holiness which it demands, but shows man his transgression. "If there had been a law given which could have given life, verily righteousness should have been by the law." (Gal. 3:21.) But as this is spiritual, and man is carnal, it can only condemn. Man is unrighteous, and therefore needs the justification which God bestows without the law, on the ground of another's righteousness.

Finally, the sinner is justified "through the redemption which is in Christ Jesus." He is declared just on other grounds than those of his moral qualities. His justification rests on the person and work of another. He is declared righteous not because he is so, but because the righteousness of the Redeemer avails for him. He is not sinless; but the merits of Christ, who knew no sin, are imputed to him. He is sinful; but he has the remission of sins through faith in Jesus' blood. If justification were a declaration which is designed merely to announce a divine judgment respecting the actual state of the sinner, the statement that it takes place "through the redemption which is in Christ Jesus" would be inconsistent with its import; for then it would involve the assumption that every condition of justification is fulfilled by man himself, whilst St. Paul proclaims that its great condition is the redemptive work of Christ. If we are justified through the merits of our Savior, it cannot be through a righteousness of our own, which would enable us to dispense with His merits: and if we have no righteousness of our own, justification cannot consist in declaring that we have. God cannot make a declaration annulling His Word and rendering the life and death of His Son superfluous. But that Word declares that all men have transgressed and are under the condemnation of the law; wherefore "he that believeth not the Son shall not see life, but the wrath of God abideth on him." (John 3:36.) Our Lord was made of a woman and made under the law, that He might take our curse upon

Himself and fulfill all righteousness in our stead. "Christ hath redeemed us from the curse of the law, being made a curse for us." (Gal 3:13.) He who is justified, is a sinner — not a just person — and his justification is effected through the redemption which is in Christ Jesus, who died for the ungodly and thus secured for them remission of sin.

The denial of the proposition that justification is a divine declaration which simply asserts what the justified person's moral state has been found to be, seems to many to involve the doctrine in difficulties. It is fancied that God is thus represented as making a declaration which is not in harmony with the fact: He declares a person just who is undeniably unjust. Such difficulties vanish, however, when the light of truth shines in on the soul. We trust that the groundlessness of the objection will be clear as we proceed. Suffice it for the present to state, that the declaration of God is in complete accordance with the facts when the sinner is justified. The unrighteous person is righteous; but the righteousness is not his own: he has the righteousness of God by faith, through the redemption in Christ Jesus.

Section 2.

JUSTIFICATION IS NOT A DIVINE ACT MAKING THE SINNER JUST

One of the most prevalent errors in regard to justification is the opinion that it consists in an intrinsic change which God, by an exercise of His power, works in the sinner. This error is as dangerous as it is common, perverting the order of salvation and depriving the soul of its dearest solace. It is important that its unscriptural character be well understood. To this end attention is invited to the following considerations.

First, the Holy Scriptures, frequently as they speak of justification and commend its comfort to the soul, in no instance represent it as a divine act changing, as it were by physical force, the moral nature of man. They often mention the imputation of the Savior's righteousness, and the non-imputation of the sinner's iniquity, as identical with justification; but never do they assert that this consists in rendering the unjust person intrinsically just. They never intimate that that which constitutes its nature is the supposed infusion of the Redeemer's righteousness into the sinner. They are silent about the imaginary utter destruction of the flesh in justification, and the fancied creation of a sinless spiritual being, by an exercise of omnipotence. If the opinion in question were a divine truth, and not a human error, this silence of Scripture respecting so important an element in the nature of justification would be unaccountable. Its reception as part of the Christian faith — notwithstanding such silence — would involve us in other errors of the gravest import. It would be admitting the claim of Rome that the Scriptures are not the only fountain whence articles of faith must be derived, and are not the only rule of that faith; and it would be assuming the blasphemous position that God, in the very article which forms the heart of the Christian system, and in the very point upon which all consolation for the sighing soul depends, left man to grope in darkness and in wretchedness, vainly endeavoring by nature to supply the radical deficiency of revelation.

It is true that Christ dwells in our hearts by faith and directs them in the way of holiness; but this truth has its proper place in the article of our sanctification, not in that of our justification. It is entirely irrelevant to introduce it into the latter, and those who persist in such irrelevancy fall under the condemnation of St. Peter's words, who, speaking of St. Paul's writings, says: "In which are some things hard to be understood, which they that are unlearned and unstable wrest, as they do also the other Scriptures, unto their own destruction." (2 Peter 3:16.) For it is by no means a matter of indifference whether the moral change, which must confessedly take place in the sinner, be referred to his justification or to his sanctification. Both are acts of God, indeed, and both are necessary. But their end is not identical, and their identification involves the interchange of predicates peculiar to each, which introduces confusion into the whole plan of salvation and banishes all peace from the sinner's soul. To the justified person old things certainly pass away and all things become new; he walks not after the flesh, but after the Spirit. We have no desire to conceal this truth from the reader's view. But this change forms no part of justification, and is never spoken of in the Word of God as if it did. "Although the converted and believing have incipient renovation, sanctification, charity, love, and good works, these cannot, and must not, and dare not be referred to the article of justification before God and confounded with it, in order that Christ, our Redeemer, may not be deprived of His glory, and troubled consciences may not, since our new obedience is imperfect and impure, be robbed of their abiding consolation." (Form. Conc).

Secondly, it is, in the nature of things, impossible that man should love God and his neighbor, and thus become intrinsically righteous, before he believes the love which God has to us. This would require a change in his nature which would be tantamount to an utter destruction of his sinful self, and the creation of a new person not identical with the former. For as long as he is conscious of his sinfulness and recognizes the denunciations of God's wrath upon him on account of it, but has no knowledge of an atonement, or no confidence in it, he can only hate his Maker; "because the carnal mind is enmity against God." Hence the Holy Spirit declares: "You, that were sometime alienated and enemies in your mind by wicked works, yet now hath He reconciled." (Col. 1:21.) Hence, too, it is said that "the law worketh wrath" (Rom. 4:15), revealing God's hatred of sin and man's hatred of God. The first step towards an actual change in the moral condition of the sinner is to "repent and believe the Gospel." But this faith implies the assurance of an atonement accomplished, and of divine grace toward the sinner on the ground of this atonement, as this is proclaimed in the Gospel. Through the mercy of God forgiveness of sins is preached for man's appropriation. If he believes not the tidings, his heart remains at enmity with God, and intrinsic holiness is impossible. If he believes them, God ceases to be to his mind a hateful object, and his enmity ceases; on the other hand, he loves God, and the work of sanctification has commenced. For "herein is love, not that we loved God, but that He loved us and sent His Son to be the propitiation for our sins. And we have known and believed the love that God hath for us. We love Him because He first loved us." (1 John 4:10, 16, 19.)

It is therefore evident that before there can be any intrinsic holiness there must be that faith which has the promise of salvation without it. The former cannot be a part of justification, because it can exist only when this has preceded it. Faith in the Gospel is the appropriation of pardon; and to speak of man's being rendered sinless in his justification, that he may receive remission of sin, is simply absurd, justification is the indispensable condition of sanctification; and those who teach that we must be sanctified in order to be justified, or that to be justified means to be sanctified, teach solecisms. Hence the Reformers declared: "Our opponents also make the silly assertion that man, guilty of eternal wrath, merits remission of sin by acts of love, although it is impossible to love God before faith has apprehended the remission of sins. For the heart that truly feels the wrath of God cannot love Him, unless He be shown to be reconciled. While He terrifies us and threatens to consign us to eternal death, human nature must be disheartened and can experience no spark of love toward an angry God, who denounces condemnation and punishment against it, until He Himself administer comfort. It is easy for idle and inexperienced persons to indulge in such dreams about love, as though a person who is even guilty of mortal sin could love God above all things; for they know not what a burden sin is, and what wretchedness it is to feel the wrath of God. But pious souls, who have experienced the agony of conscience and the conflict with Satan, know the vanity of such philosophical speculations." (Apol. Con. ii., 36, 37.)

Thirdly, justification cannot consist in an intrinsic change of the unjust into a just person, because the justified sinner is a sinner still. This is evidenced by the consciousness of every Christian the voice of whose experience has not been stifled by some unscriptural theory. There are those, indeed, who claim sinless perfection; and it is not for us to judge them by pronouncing it absolutely impossible that there should be children of God among them. But they must be blind indeed who perceive nothing in the impulses and inclinations of their hearts that contravenes the law of God. They may not deem it sinful, because they have very imperfect views of the nature of sin. They may hold concupiscence to be innocent so long as it does not break forth in wicked words and works. They may think the depravity which spreads its venom over their whole nature, and which presents itself to the consciousness with such frequency in thoughts and feelings and volitions, is not damnable.

But it cannot be that they are never conscious of any such operations as the Bible declares to be sin, whether their sinfulness be recognized or not.

Those who glorify their Savior by trusting in Him alone —exalting Him the more, the more they feel their own depravity —with one accord testify that their own experience declares them sinful still, though they have the peace of God which passeth understanding, "being justified freely by His grace." The holiest men that have ever lived thus gave Jesus all the praise of their salvation. "Let no man therefore despair," says Luther, "if he feel the flesh oftentimes to stir up new battle against the Spirit, or if he cannot at once subdue the flesh and make it obedient to the Spirit. I also do wish myself to have a more valiant and constant heart, which might be able not only boldly to contemn the threatenings of tyrants, the heresies, offenses, and tumults which Satan and his soldiers, the enemies of the Gospel, stir up; but also might shake off the vexations and anguish of spirit, and not fear the sharpness of death, but receive and embrace it as a most friendly guest. But I find another law in my members, rebelling against the law of my mind." (Com. on Gal., p. 574.)

And this experience is perfectly coincident with the teachings of Scripture, which declares the justified person free from guilt at the same time that it pronounces his nature sinful. Thus, while it is stated, on the one hand, that "there is no condemnation to them which are in Christ Jesus" (Rom, 8:1), and that "the blood of Jesus Christ, His Son, cleanseth us from all sin" (1 John 1:7), it is emphatically proclaimed, on the other, "If we say that we have no sin we deceive, ourselves, and the truth is not in us" (1 John 1:8), and "The flesh lusteth against the Spirit, and the Spirit against the flesh: and these are contrary the one to the other, so that ye cannot do the things that ye would" (Gal. 5:17). There has, indeed, been a theory devised for divesting the latter class of passages of their force. They have been represented as referring to man in his natural state, before justification has taken place, and, therefore, as being irrelevant to the question before us; but those who are willing to examine the matter for themselves will not be deceived by such groundless theories. In the words "if we say that we have no sin," the subject "we," whether we refer it to Christians or to all men, must in any case include Christians, as it includes St. John. Moreover, in man's natural state the Spirit does not lust against the flesh, and there is neither will nor ability to perform that which is good, but both for that which is evil; so that there can be no contrariety.

Dr. Luther says on the passage from St. Paul: "These two captains or leaders; the flesh and the Spirit, are one against the other in your body, so that ye cannot do what ye would. And this place plainly bears witness that Paul writes these things to the faithful; that is, to the Church believing in Christ, baptized, justified, renewed, and having full forgiveness of sins. Still he says that he has the flesh rebelling against the Spirit. After the same manner he speaks of himself in Romans 7, 'I am carnal, sold under sin,' and 'I see another law in my members, rebelling against the law of my mind, and leading me captive unto the law of sin which is in my members.' And again, 'O wretched man that I am! who shall deliver me from the body of this death?' Here not only the schoolmen, but also some of the old Fathers, are much troubled, seeking how they may excuse Paul; for it seems to them absurd and unseemly to say that the chosen vessel of Christ should have sin. But we credit Paul's own words, wherein he plainly confesses that he is sold under sin, that he is led captive of sin, that he has a law in his members rebelling against him, and that with the flesh he serves the law of sin. Here again they answer that the apostle speaks in the person of the wicked. But the wicked do not complain of the rebellion of their flesh, of any battle or conflict, or of the captivity and bondage of sin; for in them sin reigns mightily. This is, therefore, the very complaint of Paul and of all the faithful,—and those have done very wickedly who have thought it necessary to excuse Paul and exonerate the faithful from having sin; for by this notion, which proceeds from ignorance of the doctrine of faith, they have robbed the Church of a strong consolation: they have abolished forgiveness of sins, and made Christ of none effect.

"It is very profitable for the godly to know this and to bear it well in mind; for it wonderfully comforts them when they are tempted. When I was a monk I thought I was utterly cast away, if at any time I felt the lust of the flesh; that is, if I felt any evil motion, carnal lust, wrath, hatred, or envy against any brother. I essayed many ways to help and to quiet my conscience, but in vain; for the concupiscence and lust of my flesh would always return, so that I could not rest, but was continually vexed with these thoughts: this or that sin thou hast committed, thou art infected with envy, with impatience and such other sins; therefore, thou hast entered into this holy order in vain, and all thy good works are unprofitable. If I had then rightly understood these sentences of St. Paul, I should not have so miserably tormented myself, but should have thought and said to myself, as I commonly do now: Martin, thou shalt not be utterly without sin, for thou hast flesh; thou shalt therefore feel the battle there- of, according to that saying of Paul, 'the flesh lusteth against the Spirit.' Despair not, therefore, but resist it strongly, and fulfill not the lust thereof. Thus doing thou art not under the law.

"Hereby we may see who are the very saints indeed. They are not stocks and stones, as the monks and schoolmen dream, so that they are never moved with anything, never feel any lust or desires of the flesh: but as Paul saith, their flesh lusteth against the Spirit, and, therefore, they have sin. And the 32nd Psalm witnesses that the faithful do confess their unrighteousness, and pray that the wickedness of their sin may be forgiven, where it says: 'I will confess my transgressions unto the Lord; and Thou forgavest the iniquity of my sin. For this shall every one that is godly pray unto Thee.' Moreover, the whole Church, which indeed is holy, prays that her sins may be forgiven her and believes the forgiveness of sins. And in Psalm 143 David prays: 'Enter not into judgment with Thy servant; for in Thy sight shall no man living be justified,' and in Psalm 130: 'If Thou, Lord, shouldst mark iniquities, O Lord, who shall stand? But there is forgiveness with Thee.' Thus do the chief saints and children of God speak and pray, as David, Paul, etc." (JK 575-579.)

The Word of God and the experience of Christendom thus concur in bearing testimony to the truth, that those who are justified are still partakers of sinful human nature, not intrinsically sinless. The Roman Church and those Protestant denominations who follow in its erring footsteps are manifestly contending against God's Word in their advocacy of the doctrine that Christians reach, here below, the heights of perfection in which they have no sin — a doctrine that is well calculated to make hypocrites and to drive serious souls into despair. But if justified persons still have sin justification cannot consist in rendering them intrinsically sinless.

Finally, the acceptance of this doctrine would render it impossible for the soul to arrive at that peace which the Savior left as a precious legacy to His disciples. (John 14:27.) The consciousness of sin remains in the souls of honest Christians who adhere to the Scriptures and examine themselves. But if justification is held to consist in an intrinsic change, by which the whole sinful nature is destroyed, the conclusion is inevitable that there can be no justification where there is such a consciousness. Rest for such souls can nowhere be found, and is usually sought by them in a pharisaical delusion. He who knows that the wages of sin is death, and knows of no deliverance save through sinlessness, must deceive himself by fancying that he has no sin, or stand in trembling expectancy of the day of wrath. No doubt many a burdened soul has been driven into despair by this doctrine, which is as comfortless as it is false. Those who are not led by it into puffed-up self-righteousness which, proudly pretending that it has no sin, thanks God that it is not like other men, will be forced to the other extreme of supposing that, since they are not free from stains, they cannot be justified and there is no hope for them. Wherein should they hope, if there is no righteousness for them but that which is inherent in themselves, and which, in the best case, they feel to be very imperfect and coupled with much that is vile and damnable? What should give them comfort when, on account of their sin, they see nothing in prospect for them but the eternal burning? Justification can give no peace, if it only confirms the claims of the law, and takes place only when the sinner has performed the impossibility of satisfying these claims. But it does bring peace, it does afford consolation. "Being justified by faith, we have peace with God through our Lord Jesus Christ." (Rom. 5:1.) The discouraging figment that we are justified by an infusion of holiness, or by the acquisition of spotless sanctity through our own efforts, which introduces unrest wherever souls are sincere and brings comfort only to the Pharisee, bears no resemblance to the cheering biblical doctrine of justification. No abiding consolation can be found as long as sinners are directed to rest their salvation upon an inherent holiness. The weight of sin is too heavy to remain long unfelt. The conscience will not be lulled to rest by a song so discordant.

When times of earnest conflict come with sin and death, no fair delusions will calm the breast, beautiful as they may seem while there is nothing to disturb its quiet. Then God's truth must support us, or we fall. Then a righteousness without the deeds of the law is requisite to give us peace: a righteousness which excludes all boasting and bids us glory only in the Cross. Experience alone is not a safe guide in spiritual things: we must not use it as an absolute test of divine truth. But when the Word of God and our heart's experience coincide, it would be as stupid as it is impious to reject or neglect their teaching. And the Word of God and the experience of the heart do unite their testimony to the truth, that no peace is found in reliance upon our own righteousness, but that it is found in the imputed righteousness of Jesus Christ. The doctrine that justification consists in an intrinsic change, by which the sinner is rendered sinless, is false, because it contradicts the truth that justification affords comfort and peace.

It is but another form of this dangerous error, when it is taught, as was done by Osiander shortly after Luther's death and is still done by some who profess to reject the theory of creature merit, as preached and practiced in the Romish Church, that by God's indwelling in our hearts all sin is eradicated, so that Christ is our righteousness according to His divine nature. As this sets aside the merits secured by our Savior for us through His active and passive obedience to the law, and virtually identifies justification with sanctification, the Formula of Concord justly condemns it as an error that endangers souls. We are justified not by the essential righteousness of the Son of God, but by the righteousness which He acquired for us by His perfect fulfillment of the law in our stead. "For although God the Father, Son, and Holy Ghost, who is the eternal and essential righteousness, dwells by faith in the elect, who are justified through Christ and reconciled to God, (for all Christians are temples of God the Father, Son, and Holy Ghost, who also moves them to do the right), yet this indwelling of God is not that righteousness of faith concerning which St. Paul speaks and which he calls the righteousness of God, on account of which we are pronounced just before God; but, it follows the antecedent righteousness of God, which is nothing else than the remission of sins, and the gracious reception of poor sinners, for the sake of the obedience and merit of Christ alone." (Form. Cone, Part II., Art. III. 59.) Nothing can avail for the condemned sinner's justification but the life and suffering and death of the Lamb of God, that takes away the sins of the world.

Section 3.

JUSTIFICATION IS A DIVINE DECLARATION CHANGING THE SINNER'S RELATION TO GOD.

Justification is an act of God. Man is its object, but it does not take place in man. It consists in declaring the sinner pardoned, and in Imputing to aim the perfect righteousness of Jesus. The person to be justified has sin and has no righteousness. In justification his sin is remitted and another's righteousness is reckoned to his account. This is usually expressed by terming it a forensic act. The sinner is affected by it in the same way as the criminal is affected by a verdict of not guilty in a court of justice. The analogy is better, however, between this act and that of a ruler exercising the pardoning power in the case of a culprit whose guilt has been established. It does not change the facts in the case, but it does so change the criminal's relations that, although the guilt is undeniable, he is not condemned, but acquitted. He is found guilty, but he is pardoned.

1. That justification is such a forensic act the Scriptures teach so plainly and in so many passages that no man can have an excuse, with the Bible before him, for remaining in ignorance or in doubt respecting the doctrine.

The biblical usage of the word "justify" is unmistakable. When a woe is pronounced against those who "justify the wicked for reward" (Is. 5:23), and when it is commanded that the judges "shall justify the righteous and condemn the wicked" (Deut. 25:1), it is difficult to conceive how any intelligent reader could misunderstand the meaning. The intention cannot be, in either case, to have "justify" understood in the sense of "making just." In both cases the meaning is so manifestly "declare just" that no attentive person would be likely to think of any other. For the wicked are not for reward made righteous, but are pronounced so; and the judges are not required to make righteous those who are righteous, but they are to declare them so, and not to pervert justice by condemning them. The usage is the same when the divine act of which we are treating is the subject. When it is said that the publican "went down to his house justified rather than" the Pharisee (Luke 18:14), it is plain that only a forensic act is indicated. He was declared just, though he was a sinner and confessed himself to be such.

The expressions used to indicate the opposite of "justify" uniformly point to this forensic sense. In one of the passages already quoted, "justify" is the antithesis of "condemn"; and as the latter cannot mean "to make wicked," neither can the former mean "to make righteous." In both cases the words indicate a declaration, not an exercise of power working a change in the object. The passage in Matthew 12:37, "By thy words thou shalt be justified, and by thy words thou shalt be condemned," cannot mean that the words spoken shall be the means of carrying on a sanctifying process, on the one hand, and a corrupting process, on the other: it evidently refers merely to a sentence to be pronounced according to the words uttered. Passages of this description furnish irrefragable proof of the forensic meaning of the term "justify."

This signification, moreover, is suggested by all the terms used in relation to the act of justification: they are uniformly forensic. Thus the process is called judgment (Psalm 143:2); an accuser is mentioned (John 14:45); Christ is denominated an Advocate (1 John 2:1); a Judge is spoken of (John 5:27); a witness is referred to (Rom. 2:19). The whole conception is that of a tribunal before which the culprit is brought and, although manifestly guilty, acquitted in view of a ransom offered, without which ransom it would be dreadful to be summoned to the trial. "Enter not into judgment with Thy servant, for in Thy sight shall no man living be justified." (Psalm 143:2.) Whenever the process is described, the terms used are always equivalent to declaring just, never to making just. To justify is the same as not to condemn (John 3:18), not to impute sin (Rom. 4:7). The Psalmist's words, "In Thy sight shall no man living be justified," become utterly unintelligible if justify be taken in any other than a forensic sense. For if the culprit is guilty, that would be a good reason why he should be made just, no reason at all why he should not be. It is the wicked who need sanctification. But his guilt is a good reason why he could not be declared guiltless. If God would deal in strict justice with the sinner He would not and could not pronounce him just. "By the deeds of the law there shall no flesh be justified." The justification can take place only on the ground of another's satisfaction. If it were not a forensic act the whole account of the transaction would necessarily be different.

Taking all this into consideration, in connection with the fact: that the Scriptures never use the word "justify" in any other than such judicial sense, it is incontrovertibly certain that justification is a forensic act, by which the criminal, notwithstanding his manifest guilt, is declared acquitted or absolved.

2. But such acquittal consists in the forgiveness of sins. The Judge of all the earth, who always does right, cannot ignore sin, nor can man conceal it from Him. Its curse can be removed from the sinner only by a gracious pardon.

The supposition that God repeals or disregards His law, which reveals eternal justice, or that He connives at transgression and permits it to go unpunished, implies a false and an utterly unworthy conception of Deity. It is disgraceful weakness in a father who has threatened his child with chastisement in case of disobedience, to withhold the punishment when the act has been committed. God is not sinful man that He should do this. In Him pity cannot subvert justice. Sin is abomination to the Holy One, and the punishment denounced against it must be visited upon the sinner. The holiness which prompted the menace also demands its execution. He would cease to be God, who is of purer eyes than to behold evil and cannot look upon iniquity, in whose sight not even the stars are pure, if He suffered His creatures to walk with impunity in the ways of wickedness. "The wrath of God is revealed from heaven against all ungodliness and unrighteousness of men." (Rom. 1:18.)

And as He condemns sin, He will surely find the sinner. Man only manifests his folly by endeavoring to hide his iniquity from the eye of the Omniscient. "The righteous God trieth the heart and the reins." (Psalm 7:9.) "If our heart condemn us, God is greater than our heart, and knoweth all things." (1 John 3:20.) "Talk no more so exceedingly proudly; let not arrogancy come out of your mouth: for the Lord is a God of knowledge, and by Him actions are weighed." (1 Sam. 2:3.) From his fellow-men the culprit may hide his fault; for these cannot look into the secret recesses of the soul, nor penetrate the darkness where hideous deeds are perpetrated.

But God sees every movement of the heart, and looks into every dark retreat to which men may slink for the commission of their crimes. The criminal, even when his dark deeds are known, may hide away from man, and thus escape the punishment with which he is threatened by human laws. But from the hands of an angry God it is impossible to escape. "I will send for many hunters," saith the Lord, "and they shall hunt them from every mountain, and from every hill, and out of the holes of the rocks. For Mine eyes are upon all their ways; they are not hid from My face, neither is their iniquity hid from Mine eyes." (Jer. 16:16, 17.)

The sinner is not deemed sinless; his sins are not hidden; the rigor of divine justice is not relaxed. In justification, sin is remitted, not lightly passed over or overlooked. "Blessed are they whose iniquities are forgiven and whose sins are covered. Blessed is the man to whom the Lord will not impute sin." (Rom. 4:7, 8.) The apostle uses this language while treating of justification, thus showing that this is identical with such forgiveness of iniquity and covering of sin. This is equally clear from other passages. Forgiveness of sin and justification are identified when St. Paul says: "Be it known unto you therefore, men and brethren, that through this man is preached unto you the forgiveness of sins, and by Him all that believe are justified from all things, from which ye could not be justified by the law of Moses." (Acts 13:38, 39.) Our sins are remitted and we are thus justified, which we never could be under the law, because this requires sinlessness. Therefore it is said that "the blood of Jesus Christ, His Son, cleanseth us from all sin" (2 John 1:7), and that "being justified by His blood we shall be saved from wrath through Him " (Rom. 5:9). The cleansing from sin through its remission and the justification of the sinner by divine grace are the same act, having its ground in the blood of Jesus. Hence the apostle exclaims: " Who shall lay anything to the charge of God's elect? It is God that justifieth. Who is he that condemneth? It is Christ that died, yea rather, that is risen again, who is even at the right-hand of God, who also maketh intercession for us." (Rom. 8:33, 34.) Hence, too, it is said that God hath set forth Jesus "to be a propitiation through faith in His blood, to declare His righteousness for the remission of sins that are past, through the forbearance of God." (Rom. 3:25.) The sinner is pardoned, and is accordingly looked upon as though he had never sinned. He is wholly free from condemnation, and is thus justified. He is acquitted of all charges and freed from all penalties, because his sins, on account of which punishment was his due, are no longer laid to his charge.

Among men a mere verbal forgiveness is sometimes granted, while the heart continues to impute to the offender his wrong, and only waits for a fitting opportunity to punish him. We are prone to transfer such human infirmities, which testify so forcibly of human depravity, to the Divine Majesty, in whom there "is no darkness at all." God, however, forgives not only in word, but in deed and in truth, treating us afterward as though we had never committed an offense. He declares: "I, even I, am He that blotteth out thy transgression for Mine own sake, and will not remember thy sins." (Is. 43:25.) There is no actual forgiveness when the condemnation is not removed and the imputation of the guilt does not cease. But God does not impute sin, and the pardoned sinner is justified. "He hath not dealt with us after our sins, nor rewarded us according to our iniquities."(Psalm 103:10).

3. And yet justification has another aspect. The sinner is absolved from sin, and is thus declared just. But he enjoys something more than a criminal who is simply released from punishment. He has, in the same act which certifies him of the non-imputation of his unrighteousness, a perfect righteousness imputed to him. He not only ceases to be a pauper enormously in debt, but he becomes immensely rich. The blood of Christ cleanses him from all sin and renders him pure and lovely. The wounds and bruises and putrefying sores are bound up and mollified with ointment and healed, and a robe of beauty is substituted for the filthy rags which hung around his loathsome frame before. The wedding-garment of Christ's merits covers the sinner's hideous deformity. He who was so disgusting before now shines with heavenly radiance in his richness and royalty. The poor beggar becomes a king and an heir of everlasting glory.

The removal of his guilt does not place him in a condition of indifference. Justification is not merely a negative act. It not only removes his sin, but also positively clothes him with righteousness. This is imputed to him instead of the sin, which is not imputed. "For what saith the Scripture? Abraham believed God, and it was counted unto him for righteousness. Now to him that works is the reward not reckoned of grace, but of debt. But to him that works not, but believes in Him that justifies the ungodly, his faith is counted for righteousness. Even as David also describesthe blessedness of the man unto whom God imputes righteousness without works." (Rom. 4:3-6.) The righteousness of Jesus is imputed to those who believe, and as their faith apprehends this righteousness, faith is said to be counted for righteousness. "The righteousness of God without the law is manifested, being witnessed by the law and the prophets, even the righteousness of God, which is by faith of Jesus Christ." (Rom. 4:21, 22.) We have said that remission of sin is identical with justification. This does not exclude from the latter the imputation of Christ's perfect righteousness. For the forgiveness of sin is based entirely upon the obedience which He rendered to the law, and the merits which He thus acquired in our behalf. The act by which we have forgiveness of sins is the act by which we become partakers of the righteousness of Christ. Sin is removed, because the Lamb of God hath taken it away; righteousness is ours, because the merits of the Lamb of God, who fulfilled all the demands of the holy law in our stead, as well as bore the penalty of our failure to fulfill them, are set down to our account. We have a righteousness by faith, in view of which all our own unrighteousness by the law is canceled. God declares our acceptance for Christ's sake, whose righteousness covers all our sin, and this declaration, by which our sins are forgiven and the righteousness of Jesus is imputed to us, is justification. This gracious act of God introduces us into an entirely different relation to Himself, as the culprit who was found guilty under the flaw and was condemned, is for Christ's sake declared free from condemnation and an heir of heaven.

"Concerning the righteousness of faith before God, we believe, teach, and confess unanimously, according to the preceding summary of our Christian faith and confession, that poor sinful man is justified before God — that is, absolved and declared free from all sins and from the sentence of his well-deserved condemnation, and is adopted as a child and heir of eternal life — without any human merit or worthiness, and without any antecedent, present, or subsequent works, out of pure grace, for the sake of the merit, the perfect obedience, the bitter sufferings and death, and the resurrection of Christ our Lord alone, whose obedience is imputed unto us for righteousness." (Form. Conc, Part II., Art. iii., 9).

But the ground of this forensic act, although we have found it necessary to refer to it in order to render the nature of justification clear, requires a more full consideration; and to this we next address ourselves.

2

The Ground of Justification

THAT God should declare a sinner just, when he is confessedly not so in fact, seems so inconsistent with the attributes of God, as these are revealed in the Scriptures, that many are induced at once to reject the doctrine, without giving it sufficient attention to enable them rightly to understand it. They are unwilling to entertain the thought that any consideration could relieve it of its apparent absurdity. The wisdom of God is foolishness to them. But it is wisdom nevertheless; and those who will give heed to the Holy Spirit's instruction never fail to find it so.

The contradiction is only a seeming one when God is said to declare a sinner righteous without finding him or rendering him intrinsically righteous. This has already been indicated and must now be more fully explained. The seeming inconsistency will disappear if we properly consider the ground of the sinner's justification. This is not found in any moral worth or natural acquirements of man, but in the grace of God and the merits of Christ.

Dr. Luther thus relates his experience on the subject: " I labored sedulously and anxiously about the sense of Rom. 1:17, where St. Paul says that the righteousness of God is revealed in the Gospel. There I long sought and knocked; for the words "righteousness of God" were in my way, which was usually explained as meaning a virtue in God according to which He is just in Himself and condemns sinners. Thus all the doctors had explained it, Augustine alone excepted, saying that the righteousness of God is the wrath of God. But as often as I read this passage I wished that God had never revealed the Gospel. For who is able to love a God that is angry, judges, and condemns? Finally, by the enlightenment of the Holy Spirit I more diligently pondered the words of the Prophet Habakkuk, chap, 2, verse 4, where he says: 'The just shall live by faith.' From this I gathered that life must come from faith, and so referred the abstract to the concrete. Thus the whole Scriptures were opened to me, and the whole heavens also." (On Gen. 27:38, Erl. Lat, 7:74.)

When the great Reformer was once led to see that the righteousness of God is a righteousness in virtue of which the sinner is righteous before God, referring the abstract "righteousness" to the concrete "righteous" — i.e., looking upon it not as something in God that condemns the unrighteous person, but as something acquired by our Savior which avails for the sinner, so that he can escape the condemnation which is his due — the very gates of Paradise were opened to him.

Those who are willing to learn the wisdom from on high, and be directed by the Holy Ghost into the blessed truth in Jesus, shall have the same joy and consolation, and be enabled to join in the song: "Blessed be the God and Father of our Lord Jesus Christ, who hath blessed us with all spiritual blessings in heavenly places in Christ, in whom we have redemption through His blood, the forgiveness of sins, according to the riches of His grace." (Eph. 1:3, 7.)

Section I.

THE GROUND OF JUSTIFICATION IS NOT MAN'S NATURAL WORTHINESS.

It is undeniable that the human race is endowed with admirable powers, and that it possesses a dignity which belongs to no other earthly creature. "I will praise Thee; for I am fearfully and wonderfully made; marvelous are Thy works, and that my soul knoweth right well." (Ps. 139:14.) Sin has made a wreck of humanity, but the greatness is still apparent in the ruin. On account of this manifest dignity many have been led into the error of supposing that, because of it, there must be some worthiness in man on account of which God is constrained to relax His justice and let the sinner go unpunished. This error may seem to find some countenance in the declaration that "God so loved the world" that He formed and carried out His merciful plan to save it. For it is presumed that He would not love what is altogether unlovely, and that whatever is lovely in His sight must constitute some degree of worthiness. But the existence of such merit is never intimated in Scripture, all whose representations of man express or imply his depravity and worthlessness. Nor is it affirmed that God finds in our fallen race moral beauties which render it lovely, notwithstanding its infirmities and deformities. The statement that He loved the world is not at variance with the other statements that the world lies in wickedness and that He is angry with the wicked every day. Sin is always hateful, and the sinner, so far as he is identified with his sin, is necessarily hateful also. And yet man, so far as his nature is capable of being distinguished in thought and separated from that which renders him an abomination, may be an object of love. God loves the souls of men, not the sin which pollutes those souls. They are of inestimable value, though their powers are perverted to the basest use. A jewel is precious though it lie in the mire. Man has no moral worthiness that can challenge divine approbation and love. But he is capable of being saved. God made him good and great and happy, and, though he is fallen, he may be made so again. His nature has not been destroyed by sin: it may be restored by removing that which degrades it. And God, who in His infinite mercy made man for eternal blessedness, to the praise of His own glory, desired to save the souls that were lost, and formed the wonderful plan to accomplish this purpose. The object of His love is not man's moral condition, which is detestable, but man as He made him, notwithstanding the moral turpitude which has marred him.

So far is the moral state of man from affording any ground for his justification that in justice it demands his condemnation. He not only has no worthiness, but he has positive sin which brings him under the divine curse. "For we have before proved both Jews and Gentiles, that they are all under sin; as it is written, There is none righteous, no, not one; there is none that understands, there is none that seeks after God. They are all gone out of the way, they are together become unprofitable; there is none that does good, no, not one." (Rom. 3:9-12.) "For as many as are of the works of the law are under the curse; for it is written, Cursed is every one that continues not in all things which are written in the book of the law to do them." (Gal. 3:10.)

But God so loves us that He would deliver us from the curse which we have deserved. And He does save us from death and deliver us from wretchedness by declaring us just. But the ground of such declaration can manifestly not be that moral corruption which renders justification necessary. It is this that constitutes our unworthiness of any and every blessing, and our worthiness of eternal damnation. On this ground justice would require sentence of death upon us, not acquittal.

Nor can any original natural endowments furnish a claim on our part to be declared guiltless; for, although these remain after the entrance of sin, they exist only under the contamination of that sin which pervades and poisons them all. "God saw that the wickedness of man was great in the earth, and that every imagination of the thoughts of his heart was only evil continually." (Gen. 6:5.) To find in these natural gifts a ground for his justification is, under such circumstances, plainly absurd. He may be saved, but he has not the ground of his salvation in himself. He is justified, but not on account of his natural or his moral properties and possessions, or of any worthiness growing out of them. "God commends His love towards us, in that, while we were yet sinners, Christ died for us. Much more then, being now justified by His blood, we shall be saved from wrath through Him." (Rom. 5:8, 9.) The love which formed and executed the plan of our salvation was pity for our lost estate and benevolence toward the souls which suffered under it — not approval of our degradation and a purpose to reward it. "Where sin abounded, grace did much more abound; that as sin hath reigned unto death, even so might grace reign through righteousness unto eternal life by Jesus Christ our Lord." (7:20, 21.)

The sinfulness of our nature is such that it gives us no ray of hope that God will find anything in us on account of which He may pronounce us just. For not only are all our powers, noble as they are in their created essence, permeated by sin, but we are expressly told that this original depravity renders us damnable. "We were by nature the children of wrath." (Eph. 2:3.) We have not merely become so by practice. And we must be blind indeed if we imagined that the wicked nature which renders us objects of divine wrath could at the same time be the ground of a divine declaration that we are just.

"It is above all things necessary," says Luther, "that I acknowledge myself to be a sinner, as the Gospel concludes (Rom. 3:23 and John 3:3): 'Except a man be born again, he cannot see the kingdom of God.' Whoever confesses that he is born of a woman must give God the glory and say, I am nothing but a sinner, as David sings in Psalm 51:5: 'Behold, I was shapen in iniquity, and in sin did my mother conceive me.' It is as though he would say: I must be a sinner; it is born in me; as soon as I was formed in the womb of my mother I was a sinner; for the flesh and blood of which I was made, was sin; as the proverb says, Where hide and fur are spoiled we get no good robe. The clay of which we are made is not good; what is furnished by father and mother is already sin.

He who will not confess this nor own himself to be a sinner, but claims that he has a free will and that something good remains in him yet, blasphemes God and makes Him a liar, and must be eternally damned, as is meet. For he is obstinate, and will not endure the decision of God. Therefore the prophet declares (Psalm 51:4): 'Against Thee, Thee only have I sinned, and done this evil in Thy sight: that Thou mightest be justified when Thou speakest, and be clear when Thou judgest.' As though again he would say: I will not dispute with Thee, but will acknowledge Thy Word to be right and myself to be wrong, as Thou art true: but those who censure Thee would claim a light of reason and something by which they might become partakers of grace; of these Thou wilt remain clear."

Those who set up a claim to justification on the basis of their natural worthiness are laboring under a delusion which precludes the possibility, as long as it is not dispelled, of their being justified. They assume the conformity of their nature to the law, and thus fall under that law's condemnation. "Christ is become of no effect unto you, whosoever of you are justified by the law; ye are fallen from grace. For we through the Spirit wait for the hope of righteousness by faith." (Gal. 5:4-5.) The assumption that our own nature has worthiness which moves God to pronounce us just is a manifest rejection of the only Name given under heaven whereby we must be saved.

So far is man from having a natural worthiness which could furnish any ground for justification that the Scriptures show him to be full of sin and worthy of all condemnation. He is born in sin. His whole nature is corrupt. The sin of his nature is, as our Formula of Concord expresses it, "a total defect or privation of the connate hereditary righteousness in Paradise, or of the image of God, after which man was originally created, in truth, holiness, and righteousness; and at the same time it is an inability and unfitness for all spiritual things; the description of original sin takes from unrenewed nature both the gifts and the power or ability to begin and accomplish anything in spiritual matters." It is "not only this entire want of all that is good in spiritual and divine things," but also a deep, evil, horrible, fathomless, unsearchable and unspeakable corruption of the whole nature and of all the powers of man, especially of the noblest and most eminent faculties of the soul, in the understanding, heart, and will; insomuch that now, since the fall, man inherits an innate evil disposition and an inward impurity of heart, evil desires and inclinations; so that by nature we all inherit a heart, mind, and thoughts from Adam which, in respect of their highest powers and the light of reason, are diametrically opposed to God by nature and to His chief commands, and indeed are at enmity with God, especially with regard to divine and spiritual things." "The punishments which God has imposed on the children of Adam on account of original sin are death, everlasting damnation, and other bodily and spiritual, temporal and eternal miseries, the tyranny and dominion of

Satan." (Part II., Art. i. 9-13.) Where there are such depths of depravity it would be folly to speak of any merit or worthiness that would furnish ground for justification. In sinful man there is ground only for condemnation.

Section 2.

THE GROUND OF JUSTIFICATION IS NOT ANY HUMAN ACQUIREMENT.

There are some who, while they admit that our justification does not rest upon any natural gifts or worth presume that its ground must be the acquirements, which are the results of our personal efforts. That it is not wealth, to secure which so much energy is expended, nor social position which to many seems the highest goal that man can reach, will no doubt be readily admitted; for these things are too plainly of the earth earthy; they are too manifestly distinctions of a transitory character: they are, in many cases, too obviously found associated with grave moral defects and delinquencies, upon which it is felt that God cannot look with complacency. But mental accomplishments and moral achievements are not so readily seen to furnish no ground for justification, and the latter especially are often supposed to constitute a sufficient foundation for it.

That mental accomplishments cannot be its ground must, upon reflection, appear as plain as that it cannot be pecuniary acquisitions or social advantages. Wisdom and knowledge are, indeed, valuable possessions. But the Holy Scriptures do not commend them to us, without reference to their subject-matter and their application, as ends at which we should aim. "For it is written, I will destroy the wisdom of the wise, and will bring to nothing the understanding of the prudent. Where is the wise? where is the scribe? where is the disputer of this world? hath not God made foolish the wisdom of this world? For after that, in the wisdom of God, the world by wisdom knew not God, it pleased God by the foolishness of preaching to save them that believe." (2 Cor. 1:19-21.) "Knowledge puffs up, but love edifies." (1 Cor. 8:1.) When wisdom is set before us as a goal towards which we should incessantly strive, it is not the wisdom of this world, but it is the wisdom which is from above, the beginning of which is the fear of the Lord. (Psalm 111:10.) Not knowledge of any kind, but knowledge of the highest object, involving its proper appreciation, is represented as a great treasure. "This is life eternal, that they might know Thee, the only true God, and Jesus Christ, whom Thou hast sent." (John 17:3.) When mental powers and acquirements bring the soul into no living relation to the truth which makes us free, they are utterly valueless for our salvation. They are sometimes spoken of in the Word of God as coupled with a spiritual state in which justification is impossible. For when our Savior says that "the children of this world are in their generation wiser than the children of light" (Luke 16:8), He attributes wisdom to persons who are contrasted with His justified people, and in whom, therefore, the ground of justification cannot exist. Nay, we are even warned against the insidious arts of unhallowed wisdom. "Beware lest any man spoil you through philosophy and vain deceit, after the tradition of men, after the rudiments of the world, and not after Christ." (Col. 2:8.) It is a matter of experience, also, that men of eminence for intellectual ability and acquirements are often found in the ranks of those who fight against the Redeemer and His Church; that many seek only the applause of the world, desiring, like the builders of Babel, to make unto themselves a name in the earth; and that many deify themselves by putting their trust in their own wisdom, notwithstanding that "thus saith the Lord, Let not the wise man glory in his wisdom, neither let the mighty man glory in his might; let not the rich man glory in his riches: but let him that glorieth, glory in this, that he understandeth and knoweth Me, that I am the Lord which exercise loving-kindness, judgment, and righteousness in the earth; for in these things I delight, saith the Lord." (Jer. 9:23, 24.) Of persons who thus pervert their attainments to ungodly uses, justification can in no wise be predicated. A man may be skilled in all the wisdom of the world, and yet use it all in the service of Satan to his own condemnation.

Nor can the ground of the sinner's justification lie in the exercise of his moral powers, or in the results which are attained by such exercise. It has been shown that there is no moral worth in man, on account of which God could pronounce him just. But the stream cannot rise higher than its source:

the activity of his faculties and the products of this activity cannot transcend in moral value the fountain whence they flow. What is not in man cannot emanate from him. The heart is sinful, and that which issues from it is sin. "For out of the heart proceed evil thoughts, murders, adulteries, fornications, thefts, false witness, blasphemies: these are the things which defile a man." (Mat. 15:19, 20.) "That which is born of the flesh is flesh"; and "the works of the flesh are manifest, which are these: adultery, fornication, uncleanness, lasciviousness, idolatry, witchcraft, hatred, variance, emulations, wrath, strife, seditions, heresies, envyings, murders, drunkenness, revelings, and such like; of the which I tell you before, as I have also told you in time past, that they which do such things shall not inherit the kingdom of God."(Gal 5:19-21.) This fully certifies us, that the exercise of the moral powers which man possesses by nature results in sin, and that those who have nothing beyond this to rely upon are yet in their sins and cannot be justified.

It is not at all denied that desirable ends are sometimes accomplished by the exercise of merely natural powers, and that both the activity and the achievements have the appearance of moral worth. "It is taught that, to some extent, man has freedom of will to lead a life outwardly honest, and to choose between things which reason comprehends; but, without the grace, assistance, and operation of the Holy Spirit, that he is unable to become pleasing to God, or to fear God in his heart, or to believe in Him, or to cast out of his heart innate evil; and that these things are effected by the Holy Spirit, who is given through the Word of God; for St. Paul says (2 Cor. 2:14): 'The natural man receives not the things of the Spirit of God.'" These words of the Augsburg Confession contain the pure truth which God has revealed in His blessed Word, and which God's children have believed and confessed in all ages and lands.

Moreover, if the specious deeds of the natural man even were real virtues, they would form no ground of justification; or man's good works are never free from the impurities of the flesh, which he bears with him, and which affects him and all that he does in this mortal life And even supposing that they were free from every taint of sin, the acts which are performed in accordance with the law's requirements cannot make amends for the deeds by which that law was transgressed. 'When ye shall have done all these things which are commanded "you, say, we are unprofitable servants: we have done that which was our duty to do. (Luke 17:10.) The performance of duty in the present will not atone for its neglect in the past, and can therefore constitute no claim of justification. But these performances are not real virtues in the sight of God, strong as their external resemblance to virtue may be, and illusive as they on that account frequently are. For God looks at the heart, and by it judges the work. If the heart which produces it be evil, the product cannot be pronounced good. "'Do men gather grapes of thorns, or figs of thistles?" "Whatsoever is not of faith is sin" (Rom. 14:23), and God will not declare it virtue. Man may exert himself as he will, he is a child of wrath by nature (Eph. 2:3), and without Christ must ever remain such. To suppose that, with such a nature, his efforts or accomplishments will entitle him to justification, is sheer superstition.

Here the scholastics have followed the philosophers says the Apology: "and when they attempt to define how man is justified before God, they teach only the righteousness and piety of a correct external deportment before the world and of good works, and in addition devise the dream that human reason is able, without the aid of the Holy Ghost, to love God above all things. For it is undoubtedly true that when the human heart is at ease and free from trouble and temptation, and does not feel the wrath and judgment of God, it may imagine that it loves God above all things, and does much good and many works for God's sake; but this is mere hypocrisy. Yet in this manner our adversaries have taught that men merit the remission of sins, if they do as much as lies in their power; that is, if reason regrets sin and elicits an able of love to God. Since men are naturally inclined to the idea that their merits and works are of some value in the sight of God, this false principle has brought forth innumerable perverted methods of worship in the Church; for example, monastic vows, the abuse of masses, and the like, without number, new modes of worship being constantly devised out of this error. And in order that such confidence in our merits and works might be further disseminated, they impudently maintained that the Lord must of necessity give grace unto those who do such good works; not indeed that He is compelled, but' that this is the order which God will not transgress or alter. In these opinions, in this very doctrine, many other gross, pernicious errors and horrid blasphemies against God are embraced and hidden, to state all of which now would require too much time. But we beg every Christian reader to consider for God's sake: If we can be justified before God and become Christians through such works, I would like to hear — and let every effort be made to reply — what the difference would be between the doctrines of the philosophers and those of Christ? If we can obtain the remission of sins through such works of ours, what benefit then is Christ to us? If we can become holy and pious in the sight of God by natural reason and our own good works, what need have we then of the blood and death of Christ, or being born anew through Him, as St. Peter says, 1 Epistle 1:3" (Art. iv. 9-14.)

Sinful man can of himself bring forth nothing but sin, and can merit nothing but eternal death, which is the wages of sin. His possessions and performances form a ground of condemnation, not of justification.

Section 3.

THE GROUND OF JUSTIFICATION IS THE GRACE OF GOD AND THE MERITS OF CHRIST.

The ground of the divine declaration which sets the sinner free from the penalty of his sin cannot be found in himself, it must be sought in something exterior to him. It is impossible that a declaration which affirms the sinner to be just, while he is in his nature unjust and is not by the justifying act; rendered otherwise, should be made without some ground upon which to base it. God is just, and yet He is the justifier of the the sinner. The justice of God and His justification of the sinner require reconciliation in our thoughts. Upon what ground is the sinner, who is confessedly worthy of condemnation, acquitted? Such a ground the Scriptures set before us in the redemption through Christ, as infinite grace devised and executed the wonderful plan. The seeming contradiction which is involved in the proposition that God justifies the unjust is completely reconciled in the consolatory statements of the Gospel concerning the merits of Jesus as availing for our salvation. We are "justified freely by His grace through the redemption that is in Christ Jesus." (Rom. 3:24.)

God is love. The exercise of love in dispensing blessings to the unworthy is denominated grace. By sin man has forfeited all claims upon God's favor, and become an object of His displeasure. But still He desires the welfare of the fallen. He would not have them perish in their sin and be forever wretched. "As I live, saith the Lord God, I have no pleasure in the death of the wicked." (Ez. 33:1.) He yearns to save the lost soul. "It is of the Lord's mercies that we are not consumed, because His compassions fail not." (Lam. 3:22.) With a tenderness infinitely surpassing that of a father toward his erring but still beloved child, He pities us and stretches forth His arm to help us. "The Lord is merciful and gracious, slow to anger and plenteous in mercy. He will not always chide; neither will he keep His anger forever. He hath not dealt with us after our sins, nor rewarded us according to our iniquities. For as the heaven is high above the earth, so great is His mercy to them that fear Him. As far as the East is from the West, so far hath He removed our transgressions from us. Like as a father pitieth his children, so the Lord pitieth them that fear Him." (Psalm 103:8-13.) His grace is infinite as His being, and is ever active for the rescue of our ruined race.

But this grace cannot save us absolutely. Its exercise is conditioned upon the satisfaction rendered to the demands of justice. God cannot connive at sin, nor violate His truth. Whilst it is undeniably His will that all should be saved, this is accomplished only in a certain order, apart from which there can be no salvation. Those who reject the plan of God, according to which alone it is possible to be delivered from damnation, are irremediably lost. God sent His only Son to redeem the world, and sends His Holy Spirit to apply the redemption which has been accomplished. He thus performs His gracious will to save mankind. But this gracious will necessarily involves the means, without which it could not be done. If God could save men without the redemption and without its application to sinners, the whole Christian system would be without meaning and without purpose. Salvation would then be secured by a love which, though represented as divine, would be regardless of all right and of all veracity, and which, because "trampling upon all holiness and all its utterance in law, would be mere sentimental weakness of infinite proportions. Of such injurious imputations upon the perfection of God the Scriptures can, of course, know nothing. They speak much of the grace of God and its exquisite comfort to man, but never in such a way as to impeach the divine justice. They speak of God as just, and still a justifier of sinners. They represent the operation of grace as being in perfect harmony with the requirements of righteousness, the satisfaction of the latter being the necessary condition of the saving efficacy of the former. God did not so love the world that He determined, right or wrong, to save it; but He so loved it "that He gave His only-begotten Son, that whosoever believes in Him should not perish, but have everlasting life." (John 3:16.) God's love to man is everywhere apparent.

But when we inquire into the relation of that love to human salvation, the Scriptures do not tell us that divine grace absolutely determines to save men, but that "God commends His love to us, in that, while we were yet sinners, Christ died for us." (Rom. 5:8.) Therefore they speak of "the grace of our Lord Jesus Christ," and of "the grace of God in Christ." Upon His own dear Son was the grace of God (Luke 2:40), and "of His fullness have all we received, and grace for grace. For the law was given by Moses, but grace and truth came by Jesus Christ." (John 1:16, 17.) The condition of the bestowal of grace is uniformly taught to be the mediation of our Lord. "For if through the offense of one many be dead, much more the grace of God, and the gift by grace, which is by one man, Jesus Christ, hath abounded unto many." (Rom. 5:15.) Hence we are said to be "justified freely by His grace, through the redemption that is in Christ Jesus." (Rom. 3:24.) In no case is it intimated that justification ever takes place independently of that redemption. On the contrary, it is expressly stated that "he that believes on the Son hath everlasting life, and he that believes not the Son shall not see life, but the wrath of God abides on him." (John 3:36.)

The impelling cause of our justification is therefore manifestly the grace of God; but this grace is upon us only because of the atonement made by Jesus Christ, our Lord. Grace is the internal and the redemption is the external motive which prompts Jehovah to declare the sinner just. "God hath saved us, and called us with a holy calling, not according to our works, but according to His own purpose and grace, which was given in Christ Jesus before the world began, but is now made manifest by the appearing of our Savior Jesus Christ, who hath abolished death, and hath brought life and immortality to light through the Gospel." (2 Tim. 1:9, 10.)

In justification, therefore, the sinner is declared righteous before God on the ground of another's righteousness, which avails for him, namely, that of Jesus Christ. This is imputed to him, and all his sin is pardoned because his Surety has satisfied every claim against him. The process is that of a debtor's liberation on the ground of another's payment of his debt. God declares us free from punishment because our Savior has borne the penalty of our violation of His law, and pronounces us righteous because our Savior has fulfilled all righteousness in our stead. What the Savior did and suffered was all for us. This constitutes His merit, which is graciously imputed to us for our justification. St. Paul teaches us that "when the fullness of the time was come, God sent forth His Son, made of a woman, made under the law, to redeem them that were under the law." (Gal. 4:4, 5.) As the whole human race lay under the curse of the law which was violated, and as God in His infinite grace desired to save it from everlasting misery, He sent His Son into the world, not to condemn it, as it had merited, "but that the world through Him might be saved." (John 3:17.) This salvation was effected by the substitution of the Son of God in the sinner's stead. To this end it was necessary, first of all, that He should become the Son of Man. Divinity must assume our humanity and dwell among us. The penalty of sin, which is death and all the suffering that issues in death, must be borne. But God, in the perfection of His being, is incapable of suffering and of death. He could not, therefore, occupy the sinner's place in the endurance of such penalty, without taking upon Himself our nature. Moreover, the demands of the law are made upon man, and must therefore be satisfied by man. Such satisfaction the Son of God could render, so that it would be available for humanity, only by becoming one of our race. But He came to save, and was willing to do what must be done to effect His gracious purpose. Accordingly we read that the Word, that is, the Son of God,

34

"was made flesh, and dwelt among us, and we beheld His glory, the glory as of the only-begotten Son of the Father, full of grace and truth" (John 1:14); that "God was manifest in the flesh" (1 Tim. 3:16); that of the Israelites "as concerning the flesh Christ came, who is over all, God blessed forever" (Rom. 9:5); and that "forasmuch then as the children are partakers of flesh and blood He also Himself likewise took part of the same, that through death He might destroy him that has the power of death, that is the devil, and deliver them, who through fear of death were all their life-time subject to bondage; for verily He took not on Himself the nature of angels, but He took on Him the seed of Abraham." (Heb. 3:14-16.) Having thus entered into our race and become one of us, He, being made under the law, although, in His exalted person, He was superior to it, entered upon the work of redeeming us from the curse and of making us heirs of heaven.

To accomplish this it was requisite, in the first place, to render an active obedience to every precept of God's holy law, For the satisfaction that must be made, necessarily involved the performance of that which the sinner failed to perform. The law was not fulfilled by man, and must, therefore, before he can inherit the blessings which are promised only to those who obey the law, be fulfilled by Him who was graciously pleased to become our Substitute. Hence our Lord says: "Think not that I am come to destroy the law or the prophets: I am not come to destroy, but to fulfill." (Mat. 5:17.) He was made under the law for our sake, and His whole life was devoted to the fulfillment of its requirements, all of which He perfectly satisfied.

But the righteous law which our Savior fulfilled has been violated by man, and the penalty of its violation was already due, "The wages of sin is death." (Rom 6:23.) The satisfaction to be rendered involved the suffering of this penalty by a passive obedience, in which the punishment merited by us is borne by our Substitute. Hence, for our unspeakable comfort, the Scriptures teach us that God "hath made Him to be sin for us, Who knew no sin, that we might be made the righteousness of God in Him" (2 Cor. 5:21); that "Christ hath redeemed us from the curse of the law, being made a curse for us; for it is written, Cursed is every one that hangs on a tree" (Gal 3:13); that He "was delivered for our offenses and raised again for our justification" (Rom. 4:25);

that He "His own self bore our sins in His own body on the tree" (2 Peter 2:24); that "Christ also hath once suffered for sins, the just for the unjust" (1 Pet. 3:18); that "Christ was once offered to bear the sins of many" (Heb. 9:28); and that "we see Jesus, who was made a little lower than the angels for the suffering of death, crowned with glory and honor, that He by the grace of God should taste death for every man." (Heb 2:9.) Thus full satisfaction is rendered to all the requirements of God's righteousness, as revealed in His perfect law. All that God demands our Savior performed, and all the penalty denounced upon transgressors our Savior endured. The claims of the law, in active obedience and passive penalty, are perfectly satisfied by Christ.

And this was all for us, upon whom these demands are made and these penalties are denounced. This is expressly stated in the passages just quoted, as well as in many others. There can, if we are willing to take the Scriptures as our guide, be no uncertainty upon this point. Our ever-blessed Savior is our Substitute, "who of God is made unto us wisdom, and righteousness, and sanctification, and redemption; that, according as it is written, He that glories, let him glory in the Lord." (1 Cor. 1:30.) Hence we say, in our Catechism. "I believe that Jesus Christ, true God, begotten of the Father from eternity, and also true man, born of the Virgin Mary, is my Lord, who has redeemed me, a lost and condemned creature, purchased and won me from all sins, from death, and from the power of the devil, not with gold or silver, but with His holy, precious blood and with His innocent suffering and death, that I may be His own, and live under Him in His kingdom, and serve Him in everlasting righteousness, innocence, and blessedness, even as He is risen from the dead, lives and reigns to all eternity." (Part II., 2.) This is the sure ground of our justification, justice is not relaxed, much less is it frustrated, in the gracious declaration of God rendering the sinner free from the curse; all its requirements are fully satisfied in the life and death of Christ. "All have sinned and come short of the glory of God, being justified freely by His grace through the redemption that is in Christ Jesus, whom God hath set forth to be a propitiation through faith in His blood, to declare His righteousness for the remission of sins that are past, through the forbearance of God, to declare, I say, at this time His righteousness; that He might be just and the justifier of him who believes in Jesus." (Rom. 3:23-25.) When Christ's righteousness is imputed to the sinner and his guilt is pardoned, he cannot be under condemnation, though he be a sinner still; he is justified. "The righteousness," says the Formula of Concord, "which God through grace imputes to faith or to the believer, is the obedience, suffering, and resurrection of Christ, by which He satisfied the law and atoned for our sin. For as Christ was not only man, but God and man in one individual person, He was just as little subject to the law, being Lord also of this, as He was, for Himself, subject to suffering and death. Therefore His obedience in suffering and death, and His voluntary subjection, in our stead, to the law, to which He rendered such obedience, is accounted to us for righteousness; so that God, on account of the obedience which, in His deeds and sufferings, in His life and death, He rendered to His heavenly Father, forgives our sins, accounts us good and righteous, and eternally saves us." (Part II., 3, 15.)

The redemption of the human race is a stupendous mystery of divine grace. We are sinful, but Christ is made unto us righteousness. "As by the offense of one judgment came upon all men to condemnation, even so by the righteousness of One the free gift came upon all men unto justification of life." (Rom. 5:18.) Sinners are declared just, but it is not without ground. That ground is indeed not in themselves, but it is all the more safe and sure on that account. In view of our Savior's perfect merits we are freed from guilt and condemnation, and made blessed heirs of heaven, who rejoice in the hope of eternal glory.

Christ was made under the law to deliver us from its curse and secure for us the adoption of sons. In a sermon on Galatians 5:1-7, Dr. Luther says: "For the purpose of perceiving more clearly how Christ was put under the law, we must observe that He put Himself under the law in a two-fold manner. In the first place, He put Himself under the works of the law. He permitted Himself to be circumcised and to be presented and purified in the temple. He was subject to His father and mother, etc, when there was no obligation requiring it; for He was Lord over all laws. But He did it freely ... In the second place, He willingly put Himself under the penalty and punishment of the law.

He not only performed the works of the law, which He was under no obligation to do, but He also willingly and innocently suffered the penalty which the law threatens and adjudges to all who do not observe it. Now, the law adjudges all who do not keep it to death and damnation, as St Paul (Gal. 3:10) quotes from Deuteronomy 27:26: 'Cursed is every one that continues not in all things which are written in the book of the law to do them.'

"It is sufficiently evident from what has been said above, that no person who is out of Christ is able to keep the law, and all such are under it, like servants, fettered and constrained. Hence it follows that whosoever does not keep the law deserves its judgments and penalty. For this reason whoever is under the law according to the first manner, according to its works, must also be under it according to the second manner, according to its punishment; so that, according to the first mode, all our works are sinful, because they are not performed from a willing disposition, but in opposition to our inclination; and according to the second mode we are adjudged and condemned to death and damnation.

"Here Christ intervenes before the sentence is executed upon us; He comes to us under the curse of the law, and suffers the death and damnation just as if He had violated the whole law Himself and deserved the whole penalty which is due to the transgressor; although He has not only not broken it, but has fulfilled the whole law which He was under no obligation to keep. His innocence accordingly is two-fold; First, He was under no obligations to suffer, even if He had not kept the law, as He was not bound by it. Secondly, He fulfilled it with perfect willingness, and was therefore not subject to its penalty. On the other hand, our guilt is also two-fold: First, we were bound to keep the law, but did not do it, wherefore we deserved to suffer all its penalties. Secondly, even if we did keep it, we suffer justly what God imposes.

"Behold, this is putting the Son of God under the law to redeem them that were under the law. For us, for our good, He accomplished all this, not for Himself. He desired to manifest to us nothing but goodness and love and mercy, as St. Paul says (Gal. 3:13): 'Christ hath redeemed us from the curse of the law, being made a curse for us.' As if he should say: For us He put Himself under the law and complied with its demands, so that all who believe that He did this might be redeemed from the law and its curse. Observe, then, the abundant treasure with which the believing Christian is blessed, To him all the works and sufferings of Christ are attributed as his own, so that he may rely upon them as if he had accomplished them himself and they were all his own. For, as already said, Christ did all this, not for Himself but for us; He needs nothing of it; He accumulated the treasure that we might cling to it, believe it, and possess it." (Erl. vii. 270-272.)

Justification is accordingly not a divine act which ignores the sins of men or sets aside the divine law with its righteous demands and its dreadful penalties, St. Paul says in this regard: "Do we then make void the law through faith? God forbid! yea, we establish the law." (Rom. iii. 31.) The obedience which none of our sinful race could render, our blessed Lord rendered in our stead, and thus fulfilled all the requirements of divine righteousness. He did and suffered what was demanded of us, so that by His stripes we might be healed. We are saved by infinite grace, not by any merit of ours; but that grace is operative for our salvation through the fulfillment of all righteousness by our Lord Jesus Christ, not by any conflict with divine justice. "For all have sinned and come short of the glory of God, being justified freely by His grace through the redemption that is in Christ Jesus." (Rom. 3:23, 24.) This treasure of Christ's merits is prepared for all unto their justification. But not all are in actual possession of the treasure. By nature no man has it and no man can attain it. The same grace by which God sent His only Son to redeem men has instituted means for its bestowal, through which, again, He works the means for its appropriation. The sinner can be actually justified only by being brought into a living relation to Him who is the only ground of our justification.

3

The Means of Its Bestowal

THE redemption through Christ Jesus, which forms the ground of the sinner's justification, is universal; and God's gracious will is that all should become participants in its inestimable blessings. In the general purpose of God all men are justified; for He sincerely desires the salvation of all, has embraced all in His wonderful plan to effect this salvation, and offers it freely to all. But it must needs be conveyed to those for whom it is designed; and the grace which devised and executed the plan to save all through the mission of the Savior, has also made all necessary arrangements for such conveyance. "All things are of God, who hath reconciled us to Himself by Jesus Christ, and hath given to us the ministry of reconciliation; to wit, that God was in Christ, reconciling the world unto Himself, not imputing their trespasses unto them; and hath committed unto us the Word of reconciliation." (2 Cor. 5:18, 19.) They only to whom the declaration has been brought, can be in actual possession of justification; and to convey it, God has given us His Holy Word and instituted the Holy Sacraments, as the means of grace.

Section I.

JUSTIFICATION REQUIRES MEANS TO BESTOW IT.

To those who are acquainted with the Scriptures and have permitted the Holy Spirit to lead them into their precious truth, the opinion that the merits of Christ avail for man's justification without any communication by external means, or any communication whatever, will lack all plausibility. It would degrade the whole order of grace into a system of nature, and thus undermine the foundation of Christianity. By nature we have no part in the merits of Christ, and by grace we are not made partakers of them without means.

By our natural birth we stand in relationship with the first Adam, and share his fallen nature, not with the Second Adam, who came to restore what was lost. "That which is born of the flesh is flesh, and that which is born of the Spirit is spirit: marvel not that I say unto thee, ye must be born again." (John 3:6, 7.) Natural generation introduces us into the world, not into the communion of saints. We enter the latter only by spiritual regeneration. "The first man Adam was made a living soul; the last Adam was made a quickening spirit. Howbeit, that was not first which is spiritual, but that which is natural, and afterward that which is spiritual. The first man is of the earth, earthy; the second man is the Lord from heaven. As is the earthy, such are they also that are earthy; and as is the heavenly, such are they also that are heavenly. And as we have borne the image of the earthy, we shall also bear the image of the heavenly, Now this I say, brethren, that flesh and blood cannot inherit the kingdom of God." (1 Cor. 15:45-50.) Therefore, those who are introduced into the order of grace are spoken of as new creatures, so utterly distinct is this from the order of nature. "If any man be in Christ, he is a new creature." (2 Cor. 5:17.) "For in Christ Jesus neither circumcision availeth anything, nor uncircumcision, but a new creature." (Gal. 6:15.)

All that our blessed Savior achieved in His labors and sufferings profits those nothing who are "without Christ, being aliens from the commonwealth of Israel, and strangers from the covenants of promise, having no hope and without God in the world." (Eph. 2:12.) For although the Son of God took upon Himself our nature, and thus became one of our race, the participation in the blessings thus secured for humanity requires our introduction into that body of which He is the gracious Head. Without this we are in fellowship merely with the corrupt nature of Adam, and are therefore children of wrath. Our Lord says to His disciples: "I am the Vine, ye are the branches. He that abideth in me, and I in Him, the same bringeth forth much fruit; for without Me ye can do nothing." (John 15:5.) Those who will not come to Him are without the grace and blessing of which He alone is the fountain. Men are never addressed in Scripture as heirs of heaven in virtue of their sharing human nature, which Jesus also shares. Theirs is human nature corrupt; His is human nature pure. The guilt of their corruption must be put away, and the merit of Christ's purity must be appropriated. They are therefore invited to come to Him that they may have life and salvation. "As many as received Him, to them gave He power to become the sons of God, even to them that believe on His name; which were born, not of blood, nor of the will of the flesh, nor of the will of man, but of God." (John. 1:12, 13.)

To share His benefits we must be brought into fellowship with the new life which He introduced. "He that believeth on the Son hath everlasting life; and He that believeth not the Son shall not see life, but the wrath of God abideth on him." (John 3:36.) We are still under the curse, as long as we stand apart from the Savior, notwithstanding that our Lord was pleased to clothe Himself with our nature; for so long we have nothing to rest upon but our own righteousness, which is as filthy rags and only renders us damnable. When our Redeemer says, "Come unto me, all ye that labor and are heavy laden, and I will give you rest," it would seem nothing less than infidelity to maintain that we can have rest, in virtue of His gracious work, without coming to Him. To those who thus contradict the Lord His words are applicable: "Ye will not come to Me, that ye might have life." (John 5:40.)

That we, since we are not born into the kingdom of God, cannot enter that kingdom by any powers with which we are born, scarcely requires mention. We cannot grow into it or raise ourselves into it. Age, though it brings us nearer the grave, cannot, without Christ, bring us nearer to salvation. Education, though it can develop the natural powers, cannot change their nature: it never transforms the natural into the spiritual. All efforts in this direction are useless. "Can the Ethiopian change his skin, or the leopard his spots?" (Jer. 13:23.) The blessing must be bestowed upon man; he cannot procure it himself, God alone has it to bestow, and therefore from Him alone can it be obtained. But He bestows it with a bounteous hand, and whosoever will, may come and take of the water of life freely.

This bestowal, however, is not immediate. "It must constantly be maintained," says the Church of the Reformation in her Smalcald Articles, 8:3, "that God gives His Spirit and grace to no one except through the preceding external word, and with it, that we may be fortified against the enthusiasts — that is, the spirits who boast of possessing the Spirit without the word, and prior to it, and who accordingly judge, torture, and pervert the Scriptures, or oral word, according to their pleasure, as Muenzer did, and as many still do at the present day, pretending to be acute judges between the letter and the Spirit, but not knowing what they say or whereof they affirm. The papacy also is nothing but enthusiasm, in which the Pope boasts of having all rights in the shrine of his own heart, and claims that what he decides and commands in his Church is spiritual and right, even though it should be in opposition to the Scriptures and the oral word."

Fanaticism, which makes the natural faculties a criterion of spiritual things, is a more dangerous foe to Christianity than many sincere persons are willing to admit. It leaves the soul at the mercy of ever-changing human opinions and human whims, and sets aside the only reliable guide that man possesses in things unseen. And the very root of fanaticism is the baseless notion that God deals immediately with men. This assumes that He has appointed no external means of communication with them, but makes known His pleasure by direct impressions upon the human intellect or sensibilities. Those who entertain this notion can ac- knowledge no channel by which grace is conveyed. The result of such error has been sufficiently exhibited, in the history of the Church, to prove a warning to all who are willing to learn. Its products are terrible. On the one hand, we see growing out of it the wild extravagancies of those sects who mistake their feelings for the voice of Jehovah, many of whom have been driven by their impulses into sordidness that disgraces humanity, while in their strong delusion, they thought that they were doing

God service. On the other hand, we see springing from it the heartless and profane speculations of those rationalistic parties who identify the voice of blinded reason with the voice of God, many of whom have enunciated dogmas at which angels weep and devils rejoice, while, in their strange perversion, they thought them divine.

The Reformers were right in lifting up their voices like a trumpet against this pernicious vagary, and in earnestly maintaining the necessity of external means for the bestowal of grace and truth unto salvation. They did so already in the Augsburg Confession, Art. v., where they say, and the Lutheran Church says with them: "God has instituted the ministry, and given the Gospel and the Sacraments, through which, as means, He imparts the Holy Spirit. .... By this are condemned the Anabaptists and others, who teach that we receive the Holy Spirit in consequence of our own preparation, by our thoughts and works, without the external word of the Gospel." They did it still more energetically in the Smalcald Articles, 8:5-10, in which the Church still heartily concurs: "It is all Satan and the old serpent, who made Adam and Eve enthusiasts, and who leads away from the external word to spiritualism and self-conceited fancies, and yet does this by other external words. So our enthusiasts condemn the outward word, and still will not keep silence themselves, but fill the world with their babbling and scribbling, just as though the Spirit could not come through the Scriptures or the oral word of the apostles, but must needs come through their writings and word. Why do they not stop their preaching and writing until the Spirit comes upon the people before and without their words, as they boast that He came upon them without the preaching of the Scriptures? .... In fine, enthusiasm pervades Adam and his children from the beginning of the world, and will cling to them to the end, being infused into them by the old dragon; and it is the root and power of all heresies, including Romanism and Mahometanism. Therefore we must stand firm in the faith that God will not treat with us except by the external word and Sacraments. All that is boasted of without such word and Sacraments, as being the Spirit, is the devil."

To arrive at certainty with regard to the work of the Spirit, it is requisite that we be able to refer the operation, which is held to be such, to an external means as its divinely instituted instrumental cause. "For of the presence, operation, and gifts of the Holy Spirit we should not and cannot always judge by sense, to wit, how it is felt and when it is felt in the heart; but, because it is often concealed by great infirmities, we must obtain certainty from the promise given that the Word of God preached and heard is the minister and organ of the Holy Spirit, through which He truly works and is efficacious in our hearts, 2 Cor. 2:14." (Form, Conc, II. 56.)

As justification is a declaration of God changing our relation to Him, on the ground of Christ's merits, and does not consist in an internal change of which consciousness could take cognizance without an announcement, we could not from any inner sense or experience know of its existence without the Word of God. A mere fancy or supposition is too insecure a basis for a matter so vital to our souls' peace and comfort. Our feelings cannot be witnesses in the case. It is not safe to rely upon them even in matters of mere temporal moment. The fool may feel wise; the miser may feel liberal. They are deceptive. But justification lies wholly beyond their domain, and respecting it they have no qualifications to bear testimony. It is ridiculous to speak of knowing by our feelings, that we have been declared heirs of another's property. The declaration will, if it is brought to us and believed, undoubtedly produce feelings; but these cannot establish the fact upon which they rest. The assurance must be founded upon the words which announce the fact. The divine promise, not the human affections resulting from its reception, must render us confident. Even the fruits of the Spirit, which must be brought forth in the justified person, could not set the conscience at rest; for the works of the flesh continue to manifest themselves also, and these must keep the soul that seeks its evidence within, in constant doubt, if they do not drive it into despair. We must have means of God's appointment, through which the divine work is done, and find our assurance in the divine promise that it is so done, which promise faith embraces. In the absence of these we can only be "like a wave of the sea, driven with the wind and tossed."

It is of prime importance, too, for our assurance and peace, that we distinguish the means of grace from everything else which may in some respects resemble them, and which are therefore frequently confounded with them, although they are not channels through which God communicates His blessings unto salvation. The events of His providence should teach us wholesome lessons, but they cannot give peace to the sinner. Almsgiving and prayer and other activities of the Christian life are indeed necessary and commendable, and even have promises annexed; but they cannot justify the condemned culprit. The means by which we manifest our state of blessedness, and the means by which we ask for blessings and give thanks for their bestowment, are not the means through which God confers the blessedness which we enjoy and the blessings which we implore. The acts of man seeking divine favor or manifesting its possession must never be confounded with the acts of God bestowing it; and the means of the former must never be confounded with the means of the latter. Such confusion is dangerous. Its effect is to reduce the divine to a level with the human, and thus to render the former as uncertain and unreliable as the latter. The peace of God which passeth understanding can thus never be the soul's possession. Justification is an act of God conferring an unspeakable gift, and He accomplishes it only through the means of His own choice and His own appointment. These are His Word and Sacraments. The Bible names no other. To trust in any other is superstition, because it is placing reliance upon a means which has no divine promise. To trust in any other is rebellion against God, because it is an arbitrary substitution of means that have no promise for those that have. We confide in God's own means to effect His merciful ends, because His promises are sure, and those who trust in them shall never be put to shame.

Section 2.

THE WORD OF GOD

The great means of God's appointment for the application of Christ's merits to sinners, that they may be justified, is His Holy Word. This both brings the treasures of grace to man and enables him to receive them. It is of God's infinite grace that He declares us just for Jesus' sake, who satisfied all the demands of justice in our stead, and it is of the same infinite grace that He enables us to believe the declaration. Both the external offer and the internal operation enabling us to embrace the offer, take place through the Divine Word. Through it the object of faith is set before us, and faith is wrought to appropriate it. To understand the doctrine of justification we must keep in view the power of the Word in both respects, and observe, at the same time, that it is the Gospel, not the Law, which brings the blessing and enables us to embrace it.

The failure to distinguish between the Law and the Gospel in the Divine Word is one of the most prolific sources of confusion and error in the doctrine of justification. The Word of God sets before us both blessings and curses, both salvation and damnation. The means by which the former is done is the Gospel; the means by which the latter takes place is the Law. Both are divine; both have a divine efficacy; but the effects are different: the one justifies, while the other condemns.

The Law comprehends all those portions of Scripture, both in the Old and the New Testament, which make demands upon man, and threaten punishment in case these demands are not satisfied. The requirements, however, are not all of the same character. Some of the laws promulgated in the Old Testament are not of universal obligation: they were designed only for certain persons, times, and circumstances. These are called ceremonial and judicial laws. The former were given under the old dispensation to foreshadow the blessings of the new covenant, and as shadows they passed away when Christ, the substance foreshadowed, had come. (Col. 2:17.) The latter were delivered for the government of the Jewish State, and were limited, even at the time of their promulgation, to the Jewish people. Others are binding upon all men for all time. They contain the immutable rule of right, which originally was written upon the hearts of men, and which, when sin had defaced the writing within and rendered much of it illegible, was written on two tables of stone and externally communicated to mankind through Moses. This is called the moral law, the obligation of which is universal and perpetual. When we here speak of demands made upon us, and menaces of punishment published against us if we fail to comply with the requirement, we have this moral law in view. "We believe, teach, and confess that the law is properly a divine doctrine which teaches us what is pleasing to God, and condemns everything that is sinful and contrary to God's will. Therefore everything that rebukes sin belongs to the preaching of the law." (Form. Conc, v. 4.)

The Gospel embraces all those portions of Scripture, both in the New and the Old Testament, which offer blessings and set before us promises of grace. It is "properly a doctrine which teaches what man, who has not kept the law and is condemned by it, should believe, namely, that Christ has atoned for all his sin, and purchased and acquired for him, without any merit on his part, forgiveness of sin, perfect righteousness, and eternal life." (lb. v.) The Gospel gives us what the law demands of us. It -is proclaimed in the Old Testament as well as in the New, although more fully and clearly in the latter. It was the comfort of patriarchs and prophets before the incarnation, as it has been of all the people of God since. It is the only means by which the sinner, with the curse of the Law impending over him, could or can be justified. "I am not ashamed of the Gospel of Christ; for it is the power of God unto salvation to every one that believeth, to the Jew first and also to the Gentile." (Rom. 1:16.)

The important distinction between Law and Gospel is based upon the words of Scripture, in which the difference in the character and operations of these two portions of God's Word is exhibited. "The law was given by Moses, but grace and truth came by Jesus Christ." (John 1:17.) This indicates not only that the law is something different from the grace and truth of Christ's Gospel, but also that the commandments given by Moses do not contain the evangelical truth which makes us free and the^ grace which saves the soul. This is taught still more clearly in the words of the apostle: God "hath made us able ministers of the New Testament; not of the letter, but of the Spirit; for the letter killeth, but the Spirit giveth life. But if the ministration of death, written and engraven in stones, was glorious, so that the children of Israel could not steadfastly behold the face of Moses for the glory of his countenance, which glory was to be done away, how shall not the ministration of the Spirit be rather glorious? For if the ministration of condemnation be glory, much more doth the ministration of righteousness exceed in glory." (2 Cor. 3:6-9.) To explain this as referring to a difference between the written characters of the Divine Word—the mere letters of which the words are composed—and the grace and life of which that Word is the bearer, is doing violence to every law of interpretation. The mere letters of the alphabet can not kill; and the words formed of these letters are sometimes words which are spirit and life, and do not kill, but make alive. The letter which killeth is expressly stated in the seventh verse, where it is called "the ministration of death," to have been "written and graven on stones," with such an evident reference to Moses that only the blind could fail to see that the law is meant. Of this, too, the apostle predicates the same efficacy in other places. He tells us that "the commandment, which was ordained to life, I found unto death" (Rom.7:10), "because the law worketh wrath" (Rom. 4:15). And the expressions "ministration of the Spirit" and "ministration of righteousness" correspond precisely to what is elsewhere predicated of the Gospel. "Received ye the Spirit by the works of the law, or by the hearing of faith?" inquires St. Paul (Gal. 3:2), proclaiming thus that the Spirit is given only through the Gospel which is preached* and which faith receives. Again he says: "If there had been a law given which could have given life, verily righteousness should have been by the law. But the Scripture hath concluded all under sin, that the promise by faith of Jesus Christ might be given to them that believe." (Gal. 3:21, 22.) The law works death, condemning the sinner; the Gospel gives life, saving the condemned.

"It seems to be a light matter," says Luther, "to mingle the Law and the Gospel, faith and works, together; but it does more mischief than a man's reason can conceive; for it not only tarnishes and darkens the knowledge of grace, but also takes away Christ with all His benefits, and utterly overthrows the Gospel, as Paul says in this place (Gal. 1:7). The cause of this great evil is our flesh, which, being steeped in sin, sees no way to get out but by works, and therefore it would live in the righteousness of the law, and rest in the trust and confidence of its own works. Therefore it is entirely ignorant of the doctrine of faith and grace, without which, however, it is impossible for the conscience to find rest and peace." "This difference of the offices of the Law and Gospel keeps all Christian doctrine in its true and proper use."

The office of the law is not to justify, although it has a service to perform in the preparation of the subject for the appropriation of justifying grace. The denial of its justifying power and design does not involve the denial of its perpetual necessity in the world and in the Church. Its use is threefold. It serves the purpose of restraining the wickedness of men and preserving order. It serves as a rule of holy living to the regenerate. It serves to show people their sins and reveal the wrath of God against them, and thus, indirectly, to lead souls to Christ, by disclosing to them their helplessness and ruin without Him. Thus it has an office to perform even in the work of justification. For "the law was our schoolmaster to bring us unto Christ, that we might be justified by faith." (Gal. 3:24.) Not that the law can ever render us just, or give us life; not that we should, when we are justified, put our trust in the law. "After that faith is come we are no longer under a schoolmaster." (Gal. 3:25.) Its work is indirect. It shows us that we are lost, and thus prepares us to accept the proffered help. That which shows us a disease, and thus incites us to seek a remedy, is not that which heals it; but it is necessary for our healing still, because without the conviction that we are sick we will call no physician and accept no remedy. The law condemns, and reveals that condemnation to the soul, so that deliverance may be sought; but it has no power to deliver from the curse which it denounces.

Justification is not by the law, neither as the law was given by Moses, nor as it was expounded by our Savior, much as its searching power was intensified in the latter case, and much as the presence of the Gospel in all its fullness contributed to its efficiency. "As regards the revelation of sin the matter stands thus: the veil of Moses hangs before the eyes of all men as long as they hear only the preaching of the law, and nothing about Christ. Therefore they do not learn from the law truly to perceive their sins, and either become presumptuous hypocrites, like the Pharisees, or fall into despair, like Judas, On this account Christ shows the spiritual import of the law, Mat. v. 21, Rom, 7:14. Thus the wrath of God is revealed from heaven against all sinners, that they may see how great it is, and, being in this way directed to the law, may now rightly learn to know their sin, which knowledge Moses alone never could have forced upon them." (Form. Conc, v. 7).

The means which God uses for the justification of the sinner is the blessed

Gospel of our Savior. This brings the glad tidings of justification, and works in the soul the ability to embrace it.

All that is necessary for man's salvation has been accomplished. The Lamb of God was slain for sinners, and takes away the sins of the world. All righteousness has been fulfilled by Him. The demands of the law have been satisfied. The penalty of sin has been borne. There is nothing further necessary than that the glad tidings of man's salvation should be preached, and that the righteousness of Jesus should be appropriated. "Thus it is written, and thus it behooved Christ to suffer and to rise from the dead the third day, and that repentance and remission of sins should be preached in His name among all nations, beginning at Jerusalem." (Luke 24:46, 47.) "Be it known unto you, therefore, men and brethren, that through this man is preached unto you the forgiveness of sins, and by Him all that believe are justified from all things, from which ye could not be justified by the law of Moses." (Acts 13:38, 39.) Tidings of joy cannot be placed before men otherwise than by the word announcing them, and the joyful news of what God has done for man's salvation cannot be brought to its object otherwise than by God's Word proclaiming it. This proclamation is the Gospel: nothing is Gospel that contains not such tidings. And this proclamation is, on God's part, the sinner's justification, which is, on man's part, to be appropriated by embracing the proclamation. Our whole debt is paid, and the Gospel announces the fad. Its office is not to convey information to man of what God can do and what, under certain conditions, He is willing to do, but of what has been done to compass our salvation, and is available for that purpose every moment. "All things are of God, who hath reconciled us to Himself by Jesus Christ, and hath given to us the ministry of reconciliation; to wit, that God was in Christ, reconciling the world unto Himself, not imputing their trespasses unto them, and hath committed unto us the word of reconciliation. Now then we are ambassadors for Christ, as though God did beseech you by us; we pray you, in Christ's stead, be ye reconciled to God. For He hath made Him to be sin for us, Who knew no sin, that we might be made the righteousness of God in Him." (2 Cor. 5:18-21.)

This means of justification is effectual not only in bringing to the soul the truth that the barrier of sin has been removed through Christ, but also in working that internal power which is necessary to appropriate the truth for the sinner's peace and joy. The efficacy of the Divine Word does not consist merely in showing sinners the way of salvation, and indicating the means by which this may be secured. It would profit us little to have such a guide, however safe that guide may be, so long as we have no ability to walk in the way indicated and to use effectually the means exhibited. Nor does the power of God's Word consist in the solid arguments and strong motives addressed to the mind, as though it were of the same character as that of an effective human speech. This would avail nothing while "the whole head is sick and the whole heart is faint." Its power is supernatural. The Holy Spirit is united with it, so that its energy is divine, not human. It exists not without the Spirit. The power of the Gospel and the power of the Spirit is the same. To say that the Word is impotent is identical with saying that the Spirit, who does not merely use it occasionally as His instrument, but is inseparably in union with it, is impotent. The supernatural power of the Word of God may therefore, in a certain sense, be said to be natural to it, as belonging intrinsically to its very nature; without such power it has no existence. Proofs of this the Scriptures supply in abundance. "The words which I speak unto you," says our Savior, "they are spirit and they are life." (John 6:63.) The Gospel is "the power of God unto salvation to everyone that believeth," says St. Paul, Rom. 1:16. And the same apostle declares: "the word of God is quick and powerful, and sharper than any two-edged sword, piercing even to the dividing asunder of soul and spirit, and of the joints and marrow, and is a discerner of the thoughts and intents of the heart." (Heb. 4:12.) And again: "For this cause also thank we God without ceasing, because, when ye received the word of God which ye heard of us, ye received it not as the word of men, but, as it is in truth, the word of God, which effectually worketh also in you that believe." (1 Thess. 2:13.) Of the same import also are the declarations of St. Peter and St. James. The former says that we "are born again, not of corruptible seed, but of incorruptible, by the Word of God, which liveth and abideth forever." (2 Peter 1:23.) The latter exhorts: 'Receive with meekness the engrafted word, which is able to save your souls." James 1:21.) Precisely the same efficacy is thus ascribed to the Divine Word as that which is attributed to the Holy Spirit who is united with it. It calls, enlightens, justifies, sanctifies, saves, as it conveys to men the grace of our Lord Jesus Christ unto salvation.

It is on this account that our Lord, when He sent forth His disciples to preach the everlasting Gospel, said unto them: "Whosoever sins ye remit, they are remitted unto them." When the power of the Divine Word is denied, it is no wonder that people are perplexed at this statement, and that they fall into grievous error in attempting to explain it. The Romish Church finds in it a justification of her priestly arrogance and tyranny, and some Protestant denominations accept the Romish interpretation with some modifications, while others despair of finding in the words any meaning that is not inconsistent with the analogy of faith. The Romanists assume that our blessed Lord delegated His power of remitting sins to the apostles, and that by them it was transmitted by ordination to their successors, in an unbroken line down to the present time. Some Protestants accept this doctrine of a transfer of the divine prerogative to men, but limit it to the apostles personally, although no reason that is satisfactory even to themselves can be given why, if there was need for such a power in the days of the apostles, it should be unnecessary now, or whence, as no such limitation is mentioned in Scripture, men can have the authority to limit it. When the Romish claim is once admitted that the divine prerogative can, in some other than a ministerial sense, be delegated to men, the Romanists certainly, as against those who limit the power to the apostles, have little difficulty in supporting their error. When other Protestants refuse to grant what Rome assumes, and yet deny what the Lutheran Church, in beautiful harmony with the entire teachings of Scripture, believes and confesses, they virtually divest a most important and a most consolatory divine declaration of all meaning, and labor in the interest of Rome by undermining the doctrine of the perspicuity of Scripture.

The passage in question confers no inherent power for the remission of sins upon sinful mortals. "Who can forgive sins but God only?" It is not the power of men, whether in their private or official capacity, that is here in view, but the power of the Divine Word. The commission is given to preach the Gospel, which is God's absolution; and wherever the divine mandate is obeyed and the Gospel is preached, a valid and effectual absolution is pronounced, which needs only to be appropriated by faith in order to be a blissful possession. The Word of God is just as powerful and just as effectual when man proclaims it, as when our Lord proclaimed it in person. He does not, since He is no more visibly present among His people, cease to speak to us, and comfort and strengthen and save. He is with us still, lo, every day; and His quickening Word is with us still. And they who preach the Gospel bring all its saving power into exercise. This Word is the key of heaven. "Verily I say unto you, whatsoever ye shall bind on earth shall be bound in heaven; and whatsoever ye shall loose on earth shall be loosed in heaven." (Mat 16:18.) The power is God's and the means are God's: man merely plies the means through which God works, and only in a ministerial sense is the effect ascribed to man. The messenger brings good tidings from his Master and renders the recipient happy; and yet it is the Master, not the messenger, who is the Author of such happiness. The absolution is contained in the Gospel, not in the preacher.

Wherever the Gospel of Christ is preached a declaration of the forgiveness of sins, on the ground of His merits, is effectively made, and justification takes place; and wherever, by the power of the Holy Spirit accompanying the Word, this declaration is believed, justification is appropriated. The fact that a great salvation has been effected for all men does not imply, as has been shown, that all men actually enjoy that salvation. Many are lost, notwithstanding that Jesus shed His precious blood to save them. The reason of this is that many resist the Holy Ghost, who comes to them with all the fullness of Jesus' grace in the Word. The purchased pardon is offered sincerely to all, since God designed and desires that all should be saved; and the Gospel, which announces the glad tidings of the salvation effected, is an effectual means of bringing it into men's possession, not only in the sense that it declares the accomplished fact, but also in the sense that it brings the benefits of the great facts to the sinner's soul, and works, where there is no obstinate resistance, the faith by which alone those benefits are appropriated.

The justification of the sinner is not, on God's part, made conditional upon his believing. The Divine Word does not cease to be true because some men reject it. The fact of human redemption is accomplished, whether men will hear the glorious tidings or forbear; and the divine declaration announcing the fact for man's comfort is true, whether men believe it and rejoice, or deny it and despair. Christ's merits are imputed and sin is pardoned wherever the Gospel is preached; and when the sinner is not in the actual possession of the blessing, it can only be because he has resisted the Holy Spirit, and hindered the working of the faith which embraces it. He remains under condemnation, because he rejects the Gospel, which justifies. He that embraces the Gospel appropriates the justification which it declares, and is no longer under the law which condemns, To him it is indeed "good tidings of great joy."

Section 3.

THE HOLY SACRAMENTS.

There is perhaps no other doctrine of the Word of God which has been so frequently and so grossly misunderstood or misconstrued, as that of the Holy Sacraments. That they are means of grace in that vague sense in which everything that suggests duty or leads to reflection upon spiritual things is so denominated, Protestants generally concede; but that they are such in any proper sense, that they are actual vehicles for the conveyance of God's grace to the soul, according to His own appointment, many doubt and many more deny. And not only does the Scriptural doctrine, which is so full of consolation, and which is so necessary a link in the chain of revealed truth, meet with frequent opposition, but it is often even treated as a dangerous error, the tendency of which is to undermine the ineffably-solacing system of grace through Jesus Christ, so clearly set before us in the inspired Word. On this account it is all the more necessary to show the important office which the Sacraments perform in the process of justification.

That Holy Baptism and the Lord's Supper are signs of grace, few will be disposed to question, even though it should not be admitted by all that they exhibit grace. The main point to be decided, in the minds of many who meet with difficulties in apprehending the doctrine, is the question whether they are empty signs, or whether they are truthful, and really contain and convey what they confessedly signify. To those who cordially accept the Word of God as a means of grace in the proper sense, bearing with it what the words indicate, and conferring the blessing which the promise includes, this is no intricate problem. The mercy and truth of God, as shown in Jesus Christ, and proclaimed in the Scriptures, solve it at once. It would be preposterous to suppose that our merciful Father, who so loved us that He gave His only Son to die for us all, and who incessantly commends this love to us by commanding the Gospel to be preached to all nations, and thus imparting to men the benefits of Jesus' death, really bestowing by His Word what that Word declares Him willing to confer upon all, would merely tantalize us with visible signs which, though they must mean something, are without efficacy in accomplishing what they mean.

All the objections raised against the doctrine that the Sacraments are means of grace hold equally against the Word of God as such a means, or against predicating this of any earthly material. They are, in fact, objections against all means of grace, and are as futile in the one case as in the other. They merely display a misapprehension of the whole gracious economy of God. Sometimes well meant, no doubt, they are always unhappy, as they disparage the wisdom and mercy of God, and turn aside one of the richest streams of consolation. The thoughtful cannot fail to perceive the faultiness of a system which, while it supplies gracious gifts for the welfare of man, makes no provision for their distribution. To charge such an unfortunate oversight upon God, notwithstanding the clear statements of His Word, showing us the merciful provision made for dispensing His grace, is no innocent mistake that can be passed over with indifference. It is dreadful in itself and pernicious in its consequences. It impeaches the character of Jehovah, because it represents Him as not sufficiently wise or sufficiently merciful to form a complete plan for man's salvation, there being no means appointed to convey it. It destroys the' peace of man, because it leaves him to grope for the salvation without knowing where it is to be found. No such theory can, with the least semblance of truth, claim Biblical support: it is a strong delusion, and nothing more.

A sacrament is a visible word. Words are signs. They signify something. But there are other signs besides words. We communicate to each other our thoughts by audible signs when we converse orally. We write certain characters, which represent the sounds uttered in oral converse, and we have visible signs. These are still words. We express our emotions by actions, and we have visible signs. These are not strictly words in the proper sense. But they convey our meaning, and we call them language. Conveying our meaning by actions is styled speaking by gesture. Actions speak. The Sacraments are actions of God: they speak God's pleasure. They are visible words with a plain signification, and this signification is divine. God can no more deceive us by visible than by audible words. He cannot lie. The Word of God, whether audible or visible, or both, is quick and powerful.

It is evident that not every sign is divine. Human signs convey human thoughts, and have human power. Human signs cannot justify the sinner: they are impotent to this end, because man is impotent in this domain. God's Word alone is the divine power unto salvation. This word we find in the Bible. The Bible is the criterion by which we distinguish the powerful word of God from the powerless word of man. The same test must be applied to the visible as to the audible word. It is sheer superstition to attribute divine power to a human ordinance. If Lutherans did this it would be no wonder that others cry out against us. Those who are zealous for the honor of God could not do otherwise. But Lutherans do not dream of this. The visible word of God has divine power; but no other word than that which is divine has such power. The visible word of God is the Holy Sacraments.

A sacrament is an action of divine institution in which, through an external, visible sign, the grace of God is conferred, or, if the subject be already a believer, that grace is certified and sealed. Two marks are essential to it There must, in the first place, be a clear expression of God's will that a certain external element is to be used, in His name, to accomplish His purpose. External elements have no inherent power to justify or to sanctify. They can receive it only through the divine will and appointment. This appointment we have, of course, no right to assume without warrant in His written Word. We can believe that a material element will be efficacious to accomplish a spiritual purpose, only when we have it plainly designated in Holy Scripture as divinely appointed for that purpose. The natural force of the element is of no avail in the sphere of the spiritual. "The water, without the word of God, is simply water, and no Baptism." There must, therefore, in the second place, be a clear promise of God set before us in His Word that, by the application of a designated element, divine grace shall be communicated. Without such designation of the element, and such promise annexed to the command obligating us to apply it, it would be presumptuous to introduce a rite as necessary, and superstitious to expect: any spiritual benefit from it. Of such divine ordinances, in which the use of a material element is commanded and grace is promised, there are but two mentioned in the Bible, which are the Sacraments of Baptism and the Lord's Supper. These are the visible word of God.

This visible word has precisely the same power as that which is audible. When God declares, by the act of Baptism, that He is willing to cleanse the soul, even supposing that no more were declared, we have the assurance that the cleansing is effected by the act. There is no condition to be fulfilled before that will can become operative. The blood of Jesus does cleanse from all sin, and this only needs application. To apply His cleansing blood, Baptism is instituted and administered. There is no reason whatever why that which is signified should not take place now. Any objection to its taking place while the act is performed, would hold equally good against its taking place at any time. The Lord is willing now, and the sinner needs the cleansing now: why should it not now be accomplished? God's goodness is not dependent upon our holiness, and His willingness to give is not conditioned by our fitness or willingness to receive. He offers the gift graciously, whether men will receive it or not. Why not then just as well exercise the grace when the visible word proclaims it as at any subsequent period? How should we ever know, if the sign is an empty one now, when He will be willing to impart the grace which it signifies? By what means should we expect it to be offered, if the offer is not made when the announcement is made? And how shall we believe now, while we assume that now, the sign being nugatory, nothing is exhibited as an object of faith? Faith can be no random guess, and God's mercy cannot permit our salvation to hang upon uncertainties.

But there is more declared in the baptismal act than a general will of God to cleanse us. He assures us that what that act signifies, is really and sincerely intended as His effectual will at the very moment of its declaration, and that the promise could not be more certain if the action were translated into the corresponding audible words: "I, the Lord, cleanse you from all your sins." To be certified of this we need but turn to the Scriptural statements concerning this Sacrament. "The like figure whereunto even Baptism doth also now save us; not the putting away of the filth of the flesh, but the answer of a good conscience toward God." (1 Peter 3:21.) Ye are buried with Christ "by Baptism, wherein also ye are risen with Him through the faith of the operation of God, who hath raised Him from the dead." (Col. 2:12.) "As many of us as were baptized into Jesus Christ were baptized into His death; therefore we are buried with Him by Baptism into death: that like as Christ was raised up from the dead by the glory of the Father, even so we also should walk in newness of life." (Rom. 6:3, 4.) 'As many of you as have been baptized into Christ have put on Christ." (Gal. 3:27.) "Peter said unto them, Repent, and be baptized, every one of you, in the name of Jesus Christ, for the remission of sins." (Acts 2:38.) "And now why tarriest thou? arise, and be baptized, and wash away thy sins." (Acts 22:16.) "Jesus answered, Verily, verily, I say unto thee, except a man be born of water and of the Spirit he cannot enter into the kingdom of God." (John 3:5.) "Not by works of righteousness which we have done, but according to His mercy He saved us, by the washing of regeneration and renewing of the Holy Ghost." (Titus 3:5.)

It is needless to multiply passages. It would seem impossible for an unbiased mind, from the statements of Holy Scripture respecting the design and efficacy of this Sacrament, to receive the impression that it is a sign without true significance, or that the thing signified is separated from it. It effects precisely what it declares. It is the power of God unto salvation, because it is His visible word, the import and efficacy of which is rendered unmistakably clear by the audible Word. To trust in it is not putting confidence in the natural force of a material element, nor in the efficacy of a human ceremony, but is believing in God's grace and power, who works effectually through the means of His own appointment, according to the promise expressly given. So when God declares, by the administration of the Holy Supper, that He is willing to feed the soul with the bread of life, as earthly bread is given for the nourishment of the body, the thing signified accompanies the sign. Aside from the clear statements of the Holy Spirit, ill the Scriptures, with regard to the Sacrament, the whole economy of grace implies this. What semblance of a reason could be assigned why that heavenly food should not be administered at the same time that the sign declares God's gracious will to feed us? We need it then, and if God is willing to give it, what should hinder its bestowal then? Why should the table be spread, and the hungry guests be invited to seat themselves, a sign being thus given that the host is ready and willing to feed them, and then this sign be belied and the guests mocked by passing empty dishes around? God forbid that we should think thus meanly of our blessed Lord and His Holy Supper! He is true, though all men be liars. His signs are not empty and deceptive. The expectations which He excites, He always satisfies; the gifts which He declares Himself willing to bestow, He actually imparts. In the Holy Sacrament of the Altar the bread of heaven, which the soul needs for its nourishment, is really communicated. "Jesus took bread," the inspired record tells us, "and blessed it, and broke it, and gave it to the disciples, and said, Take, eat; this is My body. And He took the cup, and gave thanks, and gave it to them, saying, Drink ye all of it; for this is My blood of the New Testament, which is shed for many for the remission of sins." (Mat. 26:26-28.) Again and again it is repeated that our Savior's precious body and blood are communicated to the recipient of the bread and wine in the Sacrament. That body which was sacrificed and that blood which was shed for the remission of man's sins, is really and truly imparted, in and with the bread and wine, to every communicant, that whilst he orally receives it he may spiritually appropriate its benefits. What our dear Lord has secured for us by the shedding of His blood, is not represented to our minds as an absent blessing by a symbol of the body given and the blood shed; but it is set before us as a present gift in the very body and very blood on which our everlasting life depends. He gives His body and blood under the bread and wine to every communicant, that all may with the heart embrace the saving efficacy of the gracious gift which they receive with the mouth.

Cavilers ask how these things can be, that we should eat the Lord's body, just as they ask how it is possible for a man to be born again, seeing he is born already. It is enough for believers to know that it is so, and to bless the Lord's holy name that the happy tidings are true. He is the true bread for the soul. If others desire only earthly bread, and deny that His body is given us in the Supper, we can pity them; but we cannot permit their scruples to mar our joy in the possession of the infinitely more precious bread that cometh down from heaven. We will not do violence to the plainest texts of Scripture, and be deprived of the richest comfort for our pains. "The cup of blessing which we bless, is it not the communion of the blood of Christ?" (1 Cor. 10:16.) "Wherefore, whosoever shall eat this bread and drink this cup of the Lord unworthily, shall be guilty of the body and blood of the Lord." (1 Cor. 11:27.) The Sacrament of the Altar brings what it imports, being no sign without significance, but a divine means of grace, full of power and blessing.

The Sacraments are a visible word of the Gospel, not of the law. They signify the gracious will of God unto salvation, and accomplish that gracious will. Their design is not to work wrath or to condemn the sinner. That is the office of the law, not of the Gospel. The means of grace are not means of damnation. Baptism is never said to consign the transgressor to merited punishment. It saves. Of the Lord's Supper it is stated, indeed, that "he that eats and drinks unworthily, eats and drinks damnation to himself, not discerning the Lord's body." (1 Cor. 11:29.) But this damnation is not effected through the Sacrament as its means. God offers forgiveness of sins through the Sacrament. But those who reject the proffered grace remain in their sins, upon which the law denounces damnation. This is the result privitively of the unworthy reception of our Lord's body and blood, which was given for justification, but which, being rejected by the unbelieving soul, leaves it under condemnation. But it becomes thus the occasion, also, of aggravated sin, upon which the law pronounces its curse. The grace of God unto salvation is slighted and refused by the unworthy communicant; the body and blood of Jesus are treated as common bread and wine, which have not the least spiritual efficacy; the whole merciful institution of God for man's deliverance from the curse is ungratefully desecrated and practically despised. In this way sin is added to sin; and that which was designed unto salvation becomes

61

the occasion of damnation. The unworthy participant in the Supper eats and drinks the Lord's body and blood orally, without appropriating it spiritually, and is thus guilty of a crime which merits punishment. In this sense he eats and drinks damnation to himself by his failure to discern the Savior's body and blood. These convey a blessing, not a curse; but the law inflicts its curse upon those who despise the blessing. The conception of means of grace which convey damnation involves a contradiction: it postulates a remedy that not only does not heal but destroys. To say that the Gospel or the Sacraments are the means whereby death is brought, is to deny that, in the proper sense, they are means of grace at all. They bring justification, not condemnation. It is the rejection of their justifying grace that condemns.

That Baptism, as well as the word of the Gospel, is a means of justification, is manifest from the passages of Scripture already quoted. For that by which we put on Christ, receive remission of sins, and are saved, must certainly be a means by which the sinner is justified. But this is expressly and plainly predicated of Baptism. "As many of you as have been baptized into Christ have put on Christ." (Gal 3:27.) Those who have put on Christ are manifestly clothed in His righteousness; they have "put on the new man, which after God is created in righteousness and true holiness." (Eph. 4:24.) This involves the remission of sins, which would, on that account, be plainly indicated as an effect of Baptism, even if this were not expressly stated. But the Bible does make direct statements to this effect. "Be baptized every one of you, in the name of Jesus Christ, for the remission of sins." (Acts 2:38.) Every place of Scripture which speaks of the efficacy of Baptism, without a single exception, ascribes to it such justifying and saving power.

The same is manifest also in regard to the Holy Supper. "He took the cup, and gave thanks, and gave it to them, saying, Drink ye all of it; for this is My blood of the New Testament, which is shed for many for the remission of sins." (Mat. 26:27, 28.) All that was secured for us by the sacrifice upon the cross is communicated to us through the body that was sacrificed and the blood that was shed. The sinner's justification is dependent upon the merits of Christ, for the application of which the Sacrament is a divinely-appointed means. Therefore Luther says, in the Small Catechism, that the benefit of eating and drinking the Lord's body and blood "is shown us by these words, 'given and shed for you, for the remission of sins"; namely, that in the Sacrament forgiveness of sin, life, and salvation are given us through these words. For where there is forgiveness of sin, there is also life and salvation."

The difficulty which many find in the way of accepting the Sacraments as actual means of justification would be obviated, if they would but consider that they are means of divine appointment, through which God is pleased to bestow gifts upon men. If they were mere human ceremonies, we could readily understand the scruples of Christians who put their trust in God, and not in man and man's devices. It would be a gross sin to put any trust in such human ordinances, which could not possibly justify. But the Sacraments are acts of God and have divine efficacy. God deals with men through Baptism and the Holy Communion, and it is no indication of reverence to deny the power of God because He chooses to exert it through His Word in connection with material elements. He is willing to save us all for Christ's sake, and there is no danger that men will indulge in false hopes when they rely upon His gracious operations through means of His own choice, to which He has annexed the promises of His Word.

Section 4.

THE DIVINE BESTOWAL IS NOT THE HUMAN POSSESSION.

The Word of God and the Holy Sacraments, as the divinely-appointed means of bestowing justification, do not produce their designed effects by the mere performance of the work prescribed. They are the vehicles through which grace is offered: but the means of its bestowal do not necessarily put the subject in possession of that which they offer. There are gross misapprehensions of the Biblical doctrine in vogue, on the basis of which many are led to reject it as inconsistent with the analogy of faith, and thus unscriptural. They suppose the doctrine as confessed by the Lutheran Church to involve the affirmation that everyone who uses the means is unquestionably saved: a gross error, the danger of which Lutherans perceive fully as well as others. This misapprehension confounds the Scriptural doctrine with human opinions which the Lutheran Church emphatically renounces.

One of these opinions involves the denial of all that is essential to the conception of means of grace, and is in direct conflict with the truth which the Scriptures teach. It might seem strange that such a notion should ever have been mistaken for the truth which we confess; but the confusion is to some extent accounted for by the fact that it, too, claims what we call the means of grace to be saving ordinances. It consists in the error that salvation is the divine reward for the human act of obedience in using them. According to this the blessing is not graciously conferred through the means as their channel, but rather without all means, the theory involving no provision for the impartation of the gift.

The whole conception is legal, and it has no room for gifts of grace in the proper sense. It assumes human power to please God and human merit in exercising that power according to His holy will. The use of the divine ordinances is conceived as a meritorious work, furnishing to God the motive for imparting the blessing. They are thus rather the ground than the means of justification. The theory ascribes no saving contents to the Word and Sacraments; it imputes to them no instrumental power, no conferring of salvation. It treats them as legal ordinances, requiring obedience, and claims that obedience in this case, as in all other legal observances, secures blessings to the obedient. They are saving ordinances in the same sense in which good works in general are claimed to have saving power. The Pelagian error, against which the doctrine of justification by faith is a constant protest, underlies the whole theory. With those who oppose it we are, so far as this opposition is concerned, in perfect harmony. But it must not be overlooked that the doctrine in question does not represent the Word and the Sacraments as means for the bestowal of justification: it treats them rather as ordinances of a legal character, by the observance of which man justifies himself.

The other opinion with which the Biblical doctrine is sometimes confounded, and which is, therefore, sometimes imputed to the Lutheran Church, is that which assumes the existence of a natural power in the means of grace to accomplish the end for which they were appointed. According to this the effect is produced as it were by magic. The administration is all that is requisite to produce the result, just as the medicine which has the necessary remedial properties need only be administered to remove the disease. The attitude of the subject is thought in no way to affect the efficacy in his soul of the means used. Everyone who hears the Gospel with its gracious absolution is supposed to be in the actual possession of immunity from the curse, because it pronounces and, in pronouncing, brings the forgiveness of sin. Every baptized person is supposed to be saved, because Baptism was instituted to be the washing of regeneration. Every communicant is supposed to have salvation, because the Holy Supper was instituted to bestow the Lord's body and blood, the spiritual eating and drinking of which secures eternal life. It is not thought necessary to have any reference to the spiritual condition of the subject — the means having the power in them, in all cases, to produce the designed effect. While we insist, according to the Scriptures, that the unbelief of man cannot render void the faith of God, and that therefore His means are the vehicles of saving grace, whether man will believe or not, we yet heartily concur in the rejection of the human figment that the mere administration of these means in all cases produces the results for the accomplishment of which they were instituted.

The means of imparting the grace of God and the means of embracing it are not one and the same. The Lord has grace for all, and through the appointed means offers it to all. Jesus has tasted death for every man, and His merits avail for the justification of every man. These are imputed to men, and the Divine Word and the Holy Sacraments are appointed to convey the blessing. But not everyone for whom wealth is designed and to whom it is offered is necessarily rich; some may reject it, and some, having accepted, may afterwards neglect it and loose it. Not everyone to whom God declares His absolution for Jesus' sake appropriates it. Some reject it and remain in their sins. The Holy Sacraments, as well as the Word of God, always contain and convey the justifying grace. In no case is the fault God's that the baptized sinner is not justified. He that believeth not shall be damned, although God desired that he should be saved, and freely offered him salvation through the means which he appointed to this end. While the Bible teaches that these means always bear with them the divine power to justify, so that the subject is always without excuse, it does not give the least countenance to the opinion that the administration of the means, or the making of an effectual offer, is all that is needed to put the subject in actual possession of the blessing offered.

The Reformers, when they set forth the great comfort of the Gospel and the Sacraments, were unwearied in urging faith as the means necessary to embrace it, and in warning against the Romish error of trusting in the mere work performed, independently of the reception of the divine gift. Thus in her Apology the. Lutheran Church says: "Here we must freely condemn all the scholastics and their false doctrines, that those who simply use the Sacraments and do not oppose their operation obtain, ex *opere operato*, the grace of God, even if the heart at the time has no good thoughts. But it is clearly a Jewish error to hold that we are justified by works and external ceremonies, without faith, and although the heart be not engaged therein; yet this error is promulgated far and wide through all the papal territory and churches. St. Paul (Rom. 4:9-11) denies that Abraham was justified through circumcision, and asserts that it was a sign appointed to exercise and strengthen faith. We therefore say that the proper use of the Sacraments requires faith to believe the divine promises and receive the promised grace which is offered through the Sacraments and the Word. Now this is the obvious and proper use of the Holy Sacraments, upon which our hearts and consciences can firmly rely. For the divine promises can be accepted through faith alone. Now as the Sacraments are external signs and seals of the promises, their proper use requires faith; for when we receive the Sacrament of the body and blood of Christ, our Lord clearly says, 'This cup is the new testament.' (Luke 22:20.) We should firmly believe, then, that the grace and remission of sins promised in the New Testament are imparted to us. This we should receive in faith, and thereby console our alarmed, timid hearts, and rest assured that the word and promises of God cannot fail, but are as sure, nay, surer than if a new voice or a new miracle were given from heaven to certify us of grace. What would a miracle benefit us if it were not believed? Here we are speaking of special faith, namely, the assurance that our sins are forgiven us; not of the general faith which believes that there is a God. This proper use of the Sacraments really consoles and refreshes the heart. But we cannot too carefully consider or speak too freely of the abuses and errors introduced by the pernicious, shameful, and impious doctrine of the *opus operatum*; namely, that the mere use of the Sacraments, the work performed, makes us just before God and secures His grace, even without a good disposition of the heart." (Art. 13:18-23.)

The efficacy of the means of grace is always present in them, and is the same in the Sacraments as in the Word of God. They are divine means to impart the benefits secured for us through our blessed Redeemer. They all contain the power of God, of whose gracious will they are expressions. Baptism and the Eucharist are not mere water and mere bread and wine. These could have no spiritual effect. The divine word of institution and of promise is joined to these material elements, and this word is always effectual, whether with or without the elements. The grace of God is conveyed in Baptism to begin the work of salvation in the soul of the infant; it is communicated in the Holy Supper to promote and confirm the work already begun; it is bestowed through the written and preached Word to the same ends. In all cases salvation is by the means, and in all cases the means contain it and convey it. But in all cases the power of God thus conveyed must, if the soul is to be saved by it, be appropriated by faith. God does not justify and save the sinner in spite of himself. The means bestow justification. They proclaim the gracious pardon for Christ's sake as a consolatory fact. They work in the soul the ability to believe the fact, which is foolishness to the natural man. They exhibit the ground of true peace and joy to the sinner, and supply the power to rejoice in it. But all this may be resisted. The sinner may cast from him the glorious treasures which are offered, and thus, not-withstanding the riches of grace offered to him, remain under condemnation.

In exhibiting the doctrine of Justification we must therefore proceed a step further, and point out the subjective condition of the actual possession of the grace which is objectively present in the Word of God and the Holy Sacraments, and offered through them whenever and wherever these means of grace are administered.

4

The Means of Its Reception

THE bestowal of a spiritual gift does not involve its appropriation by those for whom it is designed. We have before adverted to the fact that the failure to observe this is a prolific source of confusion and misapprehension in the doctrine of Justification. Christ has redeemed all men, and the means of grace convey the benefits of the redemption to all their subjects. The treasures of salvation have been secured, and arrangements have been made for their gratuitous distribution. But not all to whom these treasures are offered, are in the actual possession of them. They must be received as well as bestowed. The soul in its natural condition has them not and cannot apprehend them. There is a hand that gives and a hand that takes. God extends His gracious hand to justify the sinner in His blessed Word and Sacraments. But He also creates in us a spiritual hand by which the precious gift may be appropriated. This hand is faith, which is the only means of the reception, as the Word of God and the Holy Sacraments are the only means of the bestowal, of justification. "Being justified by faith, we have peace with God through our Lord Jesus Christ." (Rom. 5:1)

Section 1.

NO MEANS OF RECEPTION BESIDES FAITH.

It has, in the previous chapter, been shown that there is no ground of a sinner's justification besides the grace of God in His dear Son. "Other foundation can no man lay than that is laid, which is Jesus Christ." (2 Cor. 3:2) But as the grace of God must be appropriated, otherwise the sinner remains in his natural state of condemnation, it is of the utmost importance clearly to fix in our minds the truth, that the only means of such appropriation is faith.

The Scriptures, in many places, expressly mention faith as such means, and they mention no other. This silence of Scripture must alone, in a matter of such grave moment, be considered decisive. It would conflict with all that God has been pleased to make known to us of Himself and His benevolent purposes, to suppose that there are ways of apprehending justifying grace of which He has given us no information. The love which sent the Savior to die for us could not withhold from us the knowledge of any means by which the benefits of that death might be made ours. "He that believes and is baptized shall be saved; but he that believes not shall be damned."

Nor are there any other means conceivable by which the grace offered in the Gospel could be appropriated. It is a grievous and a mischievous error to suppose that something must be done on our part to render the merits of Christ available. We must recall to the reader's mind the fact that the salvation of man is already wrought out, and that it only needs distribution and appropriation to render it the sinner's individual possession. The glad tidings announcing the fact of the redemption are not something to be done, but something to be believed; and he that believes them enjoys them. The important distinction between the Law and the Gospel is too often overlooked even by those who admit it to be well founded, and the result is confusion in regard to the nature and means of justification. Good news avail for us only when we appropriate them by believing them. No exercise of our natural powers, no personal efforts of any description, can secure to us the benefits of the atonement. They are offered freely, and all that we need is to embrace them. Conviction and sentiment and volition are all very well in their sphere. But no logical power can convince us of facts which rest, and can rest, only upon the testimony of God, so long as the word of His testimony is rejected by unbelief. No skill in persuasion can arouse our sensibilities in regard to objects whose very existence we deny. No exercise of will can make divine facts to order, or bring to our souls the comfort which depends upon such facts. We may deceive ourselves and we may be deceived. We may even act upon the persuasion that certain propositions are true, while the only ground upon which their truth could rest is renounced. We are sometimes imposed upon by sophists, and sometimes practice sophistry upon ourselves. But the fires test our intellectual work and burn the hay and stubble. Sophistries cannot endure the hour and power of temptation. When the mind is aroused to examine its furniture, it cannot hold as a truth what involves a contradiction, or what is a palpable absurdity. If it is stated to us as a fact that a wealthy friend has, in his will, named us as heirs to all his property, we may strive to secure the benefit of the information by thinking about it, and exciting our feelings in reference to it, and exercising the will respecting it; but, after all, there is nothing that avails us anything save simply believing it. God sends His message of mercy to us, and at His word we are to be comforted. If this affords us no solace and no joy by merely appropriating it as true, we can have no comfort and no peace. It is right to think about it frequently and well; it is right that our feelings become enlisted in a matter so cheering and so glorious; it is right that our will be brought under its blessed influence and lead us to appropriate action: but only he who believes it has it and profits by it. There is no other means than faith to receive the proffered grace.

"Some earnestly contend against the word sola, alone; yet St. Paul clearly says (Rom. 3:28): 'Therefore we conclude that a man is justified by faith without the deeds of the law.' Again (Eph. 2:8), 'It is the gift of God, not of yourselves, not of works, lest any man should boast'; and the same in Romans 3:24. Now if this word, this *exclusiva sola* (the expression alone, which excludes everything else,) is so objectionable to some, they may erase these words also, wherever found in the Epistles of St. Paul: ' through grace' 'not of works,' 'the gift of God?' etc., 'lest any man should boast?' and the like; for they are very decidedly exclusive. The words 'through grace' exclude merit and all works whatsoever." (Apology, Art. iv. 73, 74.) There is no merit in man by which he could be accounted righteous before God; there is no power in man by which he could appropriate the righteousness which Christ has secured for him. "For by grace are ye saved through faith." (Eph. 2:8.) Faith is the only means to embrace the only Savior.

Section 2.

FAITH IS THE DESIGNATED MEANS OF RECEPTION.

In the very nature of the case faith is suggested to us as the only possible means by which justification can be appropriated. God states consolatory facts and sets before us cheering promises, and we cannot even conceive a method for their appropriation other than that of believing them. But we are not left to determine the means by mere inference. Language cannot give clearer expression, to a truth than is given in Scripture to the doctrine that the sinner receives justification by faith alone.

The passages which enunciate this truth are so abundant that we must content ourselves with a mere selection. Thus St. Paul declares: "Be it known unto you, therefore, men and brethren, that through this man is preached unto you the forgiveness of sins: and by Him all that believe are justified from all things, from which ye could not be justified by the law of Moses." (Acts 13:38, 39.) The same apostle writes to the Romans: "Therefore we conclude that a man is justified by faith, without the deeds of the law." (Rom. 3:28.) Of the same import, excluding all participation of natural powers in the appropriation of justification, are his words to the Galatians: "We, who are Jews by nature, and not sinners of the Gentiles, knowing that a man is not justified by the works of the law, but by the faith of Jesus Christ, even we have believed in Jesus Christ, that we might be justified by the faith of Christ, and not by the works of the law; for by the works of the law shall no flesh be justified." (Gal. 2:15, 16.) Again, he says to the Philippians that his great aim is to be found in Christ, "not having mine own righteousness, which is of the

71

law, but that which is through the faith of Christ, the righteousness which is of God by faith." (Phil. 3:9.) It is upon such clear and explicit statements of the Holy Ghost that our fathers based the article on Justification in the Augsburg Confession, which declares: "It is taught further that we cannot obtain righteousness and the forgiveness of sin before God by our own merits, works, and atonement; but that we obtain the remission of sins and are justified before God by grace, for Christ's sake, through faith, if we believe that Christ suffered for us, and that for His sake our sins are remitted unto us, and righteousness and eternal life are bestowed on us. For God regards this faith and imputes it as righteousness in His sight, as Paul says, Romans 3 and 4."

Those who duly weigh the statements of Scripture will readily perceive why the Lutheran Church used the exclusive particles in stating this doctrine, and earnestly defended their use, as she still does, against the heresy of Rome. We are not only permitted to say that man is justified by faith alone, but we are required thus to speak, in order to express the full meaning of the Biblical statements. For, according to these, faith is manifestly the only means of appropriating justification. This is clear from the evidences which have been adduced, to which, because of the great importance of this point, we add the following:

1. If faith alone did not justify, we must ascribe such power either to works alone, or to works in conjunction with faith. But the Scriptures expressly deny that justification is the effect of man's obedience to the law; nay more, they deny that the deeds of the law have any part in producing such effect. For St. Paul says: "To him that works not, but believes on Him that justifies the ungodly, his faith is counted for righteousness." (Rom. 4:5.) "For by grace are ye saved, through faith; and that not of yourselves: it is the gift of God: not of works, lest any man should boast." (Eph. 2:8, 9.) "Not by works of righteousness which we have done, but according to His mercy He saved us." (Titus 3:5.) As justification is not by works, neither in whole nor in part, it must be by faith alone.

2. Faith alone is represented in Scripture as apprehending the promises of God. No other means is named for their appropriation. Jesus declares to

the woman who had an issue of blood: "Daughter, be of good comfort; thy faith hath made thee whole." (Mat. 9:22.) To another He said: "Thy faith hath saved

thee; go in peace." (Luke 7:50.) "To as many as received Him, to them gave the power to become the sons of God, even to them that believe on His name." (John 1:12.) "He that believes on the Son hath everlasting life; and he that believes not the Son shall not see life." (John 3:36.) "Being justified by faith we have peace with God." (Rom. 5:1.) This is the uniform mode of speaking in the Scriptures. Wherever the means of embracing the Gospel is mentioned, faith is, without an exception, represented as such means. From this it is not only allowable to conclude that there is no other means, but it is necessary so to conclude. Justification is therefore appropriated by faith alone.

3. The declaration that we are justified through grace and freely, or gratuitously, implies that it is by faith alone. St. Paul affirms that we are "justified freely by His grace through the redemption that is in Christ Jesus." (Rom. 3:24.) "Now to him that works is the reward not reckoned of grace, but of debt. But to him that works not, but believes on Him that justifies the ungodly, his faith is counted for righteousness." (Rom. 4:4, 5.) "And if by grace, then is it no more of works: otherwise grace is no more grace. But if it be of works, then is it no more of grace: otherwise work is no more work." (Rom 11:6.) There can be no desert required on our part to secure justification, for then this would not be a free gift of God's grace. What God is presumed to owe us in consideration of our supposed merit cannot, without involving a contradiction, be thought a gratuitous gift. He bestows justification freely and graciously; therefore it must be by faith alone, without the deeds of the law.

4. If anything besides faith were required to justify the sinner, it could not be said that every believer is justified and saved. For if faith is not the only means of appropriating justifying grace, certainly some who have faith would be found without the other necessary qualities, and accordingly would not be justified. But the Scriptures assert that all who have faith are justified and saved, no other quality being represented as necessary. "For God so loved the world that He gave His only-begotten Son, that whosoever believes in Him

should not perish, but have everlasting life." (John 3:16.) "To Him give all the prophets witness, that through His name whosoever believes in Him shall receive remission of sins." (Acts 10:43.) "I am not ashamed of the Gospel of Christ; for it is the power of God unto salvation to everyone that believes." (Rom. 1:16.) As every one that believes is declared to be justified, it is evident that faith alone appropriates the grace of justification.

5. To this must be added, the earnest warnings which it pleased the Holy Ghost, by exhibiting the pernicious consequences of such procedure, to give us against substituting any other means for faith. "For if they which are of the law be heirs," says St. Paul, "faith is made void, and the promise made of none effect." (Gal. 4:14.) If there were any other means of securing justification, then faith, of which the Gospel speaks so much, would be futile, and the cheering promises which faith embraces would be a dear delusion. "But the Scripture hath concluded all under sin, that the promise by faith of Jesus Christ might be given to them that believe." (Gal. 3:22.) That promise is not a delusion, but a precious reality, and faith appropriates it to the soul's unspeakable comfort. Those who seek some other means of justification are pursuing a perilous path. Words of more solemn import cannot be uttered than those which the apostle addresses to such self-deceivers: "Christ is become of no effect unto you, whosoever of you are justified by the law; ye are fallen from grace. For we through the Spirit wait for the hope of righteousness by faith." (Gal. 5:4, 5.) Those who seek to be justified by some other means than faith make faith void, nullify the gracious promise, make Christ of no effect to themselves, and fall from grace. Therefore justification must be by faith alone.

Against the plain and explicit teaching of Scripture, objections are made by some persons, on the ground that St. James seems to point out another means of justification when he says: "But wilt thou know, O man, that faith without works is dead? Was not Abraham our father justified by works, when he had offered Isaac his son upon the altar? Seest thou how faith wrought with his works, and by works was faith made perfect? And the Scripture was fulfilled which saith, Abraham believed God, and it was imputed unto him for righteousness; and he was called the friend of God. Ye see then how that by works a man is justified, and not by faith only." (James 2:20-24.) This appears to be in conflict with the doctrine which has been presented as the explicit teaching of the Bible, and the Romanists have not failed to make the best possible use of the seeming discrepancy to bring the consolatory doctrine of justification by faith into disrepute. But the truth of God shall stand in spite of all assaults.

It is unquestionably a sound principle of Biblical interpretation that two passages of the Scriptures cannot be fully assumed to contradict each other. The Holy Ghost cannot move one author to write what is in conflict with that which He has dictated to another The passages in which He has expressed the doctrine of the sinner's justification by faith are as abundant and as clear as those stating any doctrine of the Christian system. These cannot, without doing violence to a law of interpretation which commends itself as just to every reasonable person, be invalidated. The single passage in St. James must be explained in harmony with the numerous texts which it seems to contradict, according to the apostolic rule: "Let us prophesy according to the proportion of faith." (Rom. 12:6.) Such an explanation can be given without doing violence to the words of St. James, and without subjecting ourselves to the charge of wresting the Scriptures.

Let it be distinctly understood, what is so plain in the argumentation of the chapter before us, that St. James is contending against all hollow pretenses and heartless words. He condemns the feigned faith which shows partiality to the rich and despises the poor. He shows that all professions which are denied in practice are thus convicted of hypocrisy. He exhibits the difference between saying that we have faith and proving that we have it by corresponding deeds. "What doth it profit, my brethren, though a man say he hath faith, and have not works? Can faith save him?" The reference here is obviously not to the living faith which embraces Christ and which works by love, but to the pretended faith which has not works. Can such faith save the soul? It is the sheerest delusion to assume that it can; and against this dangerous delusion the apostle raises his voice in warning. "If a brother or a sister be naked, and destitute of daily food, and one of you say unto them, Depart in peace, be ye warmed and filled; notwithstanding ye give them not those things which are needful to the body; what doth it profit? Even so faith, if it hath not works, is dead, being alone." Such a faith profits no one: it blesses no object and secures no blessing for the subject. It is faith in profession, but not in fact It is a dead thing which embraces not Christ and labors not for the welfare of man. It does not justify. If anyone should comfort himself with it, because it accepts the existence of a God, he is informed that this is a false hope, as it rests upon a dead faith. "Thou believest that there is one God: thou doest well: the devils also believe, and tremble." The belief in the existence of one God does not constitute a living faith which saves the soul: it may be a mere historical credence, and it certainly is nothing more than this when it is unaccompanied by works that glorify God's name. A faith without works is dead, and cannot save. To such a faith St. Paul would be as far from ascribing justification as St. James. So far there is manifestly not the least discrepancy between them. But this would not appear to solve the whole difficulty; for justification is not only denied of such a dead faith, but it is affirmed of works. Upon a superficial view this might be thought to indicate that the purpose of St. James is to deny of all faith, whether living or dead, that it justifies. A closer examination, however, will show that this is by no means the case. He does, indeed, claim that "by works a man is justified, and not by faith only." But all depends upon the application which is made of the word justify. The term designates an act of man as well as an act of God. The conditions must of course vary with the diversity in the application. In all cases the word means to pronounce just. But justification in the sight of man implies something which it does not involve when it designates our relation to God. The reason of this is that God sees the heart, whilst man does not. Faith alone justifies in the sight of God: no deeds of the law are necessary. This alone ought to suffice also in the sight of those who are the children of God, and who conform their judgment to that of their Father. But not all are children of God, who as such heartily adopt God's judgment. And those who are His children cannot look into the soul, as God can, and there discern the existence of faith, independently of any manifestations. They must judge from appearances. Faith, if it be the living, active power which embraces the righteousness of Christ, works by love. The works which are thus brought forth are the marks by which men judge of its existence. Where they are found the person is pronounced just, because the evidences of justifying faith are furnished. Without them no justification can take place in the sight of man, because no knowledge can be had of the presence of the faith which justifies.

To this St. James refers. His whole argumentation indicates that he has the external appearance in view. A dead faith, having no works, does not justify. But the living faith which does justify, is shown by works. Where these are, man fairly concludes that justification has ensued: the testimony is presented by which a living faith is known to exist. God needs no such testimony, but man manifestly does. In the sight of man works are necessary to justify, because not the saying that we believe, but the actual believing with the heart justifies, and this actual believing is known to us only by the works which it produces. The readiness of Abraham to sacrifice his son proved the sincerity of his faith; it could not, after such evidence that it was a living power, be considered a mere external profession without vitality. In man's estimation he was justified by works; that is, his works were the means of man's knowing him to be justified, and thus the ground of pronouncing him just. The sign is put for the instrumental cause, which is invisible to man. Thus, "was not Abraham our father justified by works, when he had offered Isaac his son upon the altar?" The profession of faith is necessary, otherwise a laudable act might, without violating the rule of charity, be ascribed to a natural motive; but the profession alone is insufficient, as that would be considered hypocritical if corresponding works were wanting. The evidence of justification is complete only where both are united. "Seest thou how faith wrought with his works, and by works was faith made perfect?" Faith must remain imperfect in man's sight until its evidence is furnished in works.

That this is the meaning of St. James is rendered certain by the twenty-third verse: "And the Scripture was fulfilled which saith, Abraham believed God, and it was imputed unto him for righteousness." The justification before God was by faith alone, and this was openly shown before man by the works in which faith was manifested. The words which are represented by the papists as standing in conflict with the Scriptural doctrine of Justification by faith are, therefore, according to the context to be explained thus: "Ye see then how that by works a man is justified," in the sight of man, who cannot otherwise be assured of the existence of a living faith, "and not by faith only," which, as far as man can judge, is a mere dead thing when the evidence of vitality is not furnished by works. Before men, who cannot see into the heart, and who therefore regard a faith as merely pretended as long as it is not proved to be living, works are necessary to justification. Even St. Paul, who urges justification by faith alone with such frequency and such energy, expresses the same thought when he says: "If Abraham were justified by works he hath whereof to glory, but not before God." (Rom. 4:2.) The doctrine of St. James is in no respect in conflict with the teaching of the other Scriptures that, in the sight of God, the sinner is justified by faith alone.

Section 3.

NO CONDITION TO BE FULFILLED BEFORE FAITH AVAILS.

Because the way of salvation, when it is represented as consisting simply in the impartation of the merits of Christ and their appropriation by faith, seems so easy, many doubt and many positively reject it. It appears to them that too little is thus required of the sinner, and that the demand made upon him bears no adequate proportion to the iniquities laid to his charge. It seems like making restitution in words for material treasures embezzled. For this reason it is supposed that, although faith be admitted to be the means of appropriating the gift, this can be so only under certain conditions, the fulfillment of which implies a moral change in the subject, so that this change is just as essential to justification as the faith which is said to appropriate it. The presumption is that the believer is justified, provided that the legal requirements made upon him are at least to some extent fulfilled.

In reference to this whole scheme of thought, it is, first of all, to be observed, that the Scriptural doctrine of Justification does not rest upon any expiation or atonement to be made by the sinner The Bible does not teach that the culprit, as a condition of his acquittal, must himself furnish something in the nature of a ransom or restitution. This has been offered by our blessed Lord, who "came not to be ministered unto, but to minister, and to give His life a ransom for many." (Mat. 20:28.) The failure to recognize this opens, the way for "damnable heresies." A theory of justification in which the redemption through Christ Jesus is ignored is not entitled to the predicate Christian. It lacks all that is essential in the Christian system. And yet this radical mistake is made with startling frequency. If it did not lurk in the minds of those who, on the ground of the inadequacy of the sacrifice and satisfaction supposed to be involved in faith, object to the Biblical doctrine, such an objection could never be urged. When the sacrifice of Christ is once acknowledged, no other will be deemed necessary, and the thought will never be permitted to enter the mind that the sinner's justification is secured at too small a price. The cost was infinite; and it is a signal manifestation of human folly, and a gross insult to Him who paid the stupendous price for our ransom, to endeavor to gild its gold by overlaying it with the tinsel of our righteousness.

Something more, indeed, is requisite to justification than a mere assent to Biblical statements; but faith alone appropriates the blessings which Christ has secured, and which are freely offered through the means of grace. No conditions are required in the subject, the failure to fulfill which renders faith ineffectual. The sinner's condition may be as it will, if he has true faith which embraces Christ, he is justified, and it is well with him.

To speak of a certain degree of sanctification as necessary to render faith acceptable to God, or of a certain number of self-denying performances as requisite to induce God to look with complacency upon the believer in Jesus, is to set aside the atonement, and to wrest the Scriptures to our own destruction. God's declaration justifying the sinner is unconditional. The condition which was necessary before the declaration could be made, has been fulfilled in the Lamb of God, who taketh away the sins of the world. There is no other mentioned. Not even faith is a condition of the declaration. God offers the gift whether we believe or disbelieve. He sets it before us in His Word and Sacraments, that we may believe it. Faith is the condition merely of our possessing the gift, and it is so because it is the only means of appropriating it. No holiness of heart and life can apprehend it. Indeed, it is graciously bestowed as a free gift, because man has not the holiness which the law requires, and therefore needs it. If we had the holiness to render us acceptable to God, the free gift of another's holiness were needless: we would be justified by the deeds of the law, and could dispense with the righteousness of God by faith.

All such notions about conditions to be fulfilled before faith avails, only darken counsel, disparage Christ, and destroy our peace. They all rest upon the pernicious error, which has its birth in human pride, that man must be his own deliverer from death; and they all lead to the destruction of that peace which the soul can have in Jesus alone as the perfect Savior. "Remission of sin is promised for Christ's sake. Therefore no one can obtain it unless by faith alone. For no one can take hold of the promise or participate in it except through faith only. Romans 4:16: 'Therefore it is of faith, that it might be by grace; to the end the promise might be sure.' Precisely as if he should say, that if our salvation and righteousness depended upon our own merit, the promise of God would be uncertain and useless to us; for we never would know with certainty when our merits would suffice. The pious heart and Christian conscience know this full well, and would not for a thousand worlds that our salvation depended upon ourselves. Paul agrees with this view (Gal. 3:22): 'The Scripture hath concluded all under sin, that the promise by faith of Jesus Christ might be given to them that believe. Here Paul casts aside all our merit; for he says that we are worthy of death and concluded under sin; he calls to mind the divine promises, by which alone we can obtain the forgiveness of sin; and further adds how we become participants of the promise — namely, by faith. This argument, drawn by Paul from the very nature of the divine promise — namely, that as God's promise is certain and must remain sure, as it will not fail to do, remission of sin cannot proceed from our merit, else it would be uncertain, and we could not know when our merits would suffice — yes, I say, this argument, this foundation, is a firm rock; it is perhaps the strongest in all the writings of St. Paul, and is often repeated and quoted in all the Epistles. No one on earth will ever be able to devise, invent, or contrive anything by which this argument alone, even if there were no other, could be overthrown. Nor will the pious and conscientious Christian by any means permit himself to be led away from the position, that we receive remission of sins by faith alone, for the sake of Christ's merits. For in this they have a sure, firm, eternal consolation against sin and the devil, death and hell; while everything else rests on a sandy foundation and is insufficient in the hour of temptation." (Apology iv. 84, 85.) The believer appropriates the righteousness of Christ set before him in the word of the Gospel; and as that is perfect and is offered freely and fully, no condition need be fulfilled on his part to make it available and to secure its comfort. Faith apprehends and possesses all.

Section 4.

THE NATURE OF JUSTIFYING FAITH.

There are three elements indicated in Scripture as constituting saving faith; namely, knowledge, assent, and confidence. The faith which justifies cannot exist in the absence of any one of them, as each of them is a necessary constituent.

1. The object of faith must be known, before justification can be appropriated. It is an error, devised to justify ignorance and to prevent souls from becoming uneasy under it, that an implicit faith, which is content with declaring its belief in what the Church believes, is sufficient. Whether the soul really embraces what is confessed by the Church, it cannot know without knowing what it is that the Church confesses. All such pretenses are mere manifestations of the heart's indifference. That a pious person is disposed to accept, with a presumption of its truth, everything that ecclesiastical authority imposes, may be true; but this disposition is clearly distinguishable from the actual reception of that which is so promulgated, and must not be confounded with it. The mistake may be made that the Church has power to control the conscience, and thus, by her supreme authority, bind upon it whatever she may see fit as articles of faith; but the actual submission has not, in any given case, taken place before that which is alleged to be binding has been made

known. It frequently happens that general propositions are accepted, but are again renounced as soon as that which is implied in them becomes apparent. The disposition to accept the deliverances of the Church might be overcome by a clear consciousness of their character. But even if this were in no case the result, the heart cannot fairly, under any circumstances, be said to have approved and placed its confidence in that which has never been known. Faith never extends beyond the object of its knowledge, though the heart may be in a condition which insures an increase of faith, commensurate with the increase of knowledge respecting its proper object. There is an illusion by which many Protestants are misled, and which is similar in its nature to the implicit faith of the Romish Church. The mere belief of the truthfulness of the Bible is frequently represented as identical with the believing reception of the truth which the Bible contains. It is tacitly assumed that the one article of the credibility of the Holy Scriptures embraces all other articles of the Christian faith, and that an explicit knowledge of its contents is therefore not essential to faith. We have thus, though in another form, the implicit faith, which exerts such a pernicious influence upon the adherents of Rome, transformed to Protestant ground. Certainly there is not the same slavishness, nor the same danger, when the Bible is substituted for the Church as the object of this faith which embraces truths only by implication. No one who is directed by the Holy Spirit could ever be led, by acquaintance with what is implied, to renounce the proposition that the Bible is true. But this does not render the principle harmless in this application. For a person may hold the Scriptures to be true, and still know so little of their contents that faith in Jesus, whom they alone set before us as the Savior, is impossible, because of his ignorance; and he may, without renouncing his belief in the veracity of the Bible, deny fundamental truths contained in it, and thus declare his general faith nugatory. The true believer has implicit faith in all that the Bible teaches; but faith simply in the truthfulness of the Bible does not imply faith in all its truth. Actually each one believes only so much as he knows, though potentially every true believer embraces all. To increase knowledge of its object is to increase faith in its extent. To have no knowledge is to have no faith, of which revelation is the correlative. Faith is not a phantom floating vaguely in the soul, but a power wrought by the Spirit, clinging to the truth of the Word given by inspiration, without which it cannot have being.

The necessity of knowledge as an element of saving faith is frequently exhibited in Scripture. Our Lord declares: "This is life eternal, that they might know Thee, the only true God, and Jesus Christ, whom Thou hast sent." (John 17:3.) Those who speak disparagingly of knowledge and pronounce it useless, if not injurious in spiritual matters, are prone to point in triumph to the fad that mere intellectual apprehension cannot be meant in this passage. Certainly mere knowing, in that sense, cannot be eternal life. But it is manifest that, although the word implies in this passage that which in the believer's heart is a necessary concomitant of knowledge, it does not, on this account, lose its proper signification. It means knowledge, although, being used synecdochically, it means something in addition to that which the term usually signifies. St Paul writes: "This I say therefore, and testify in the Lord, that ye henceforth walk not as other Gentiles walk, in the vanity of their mind, having the understanding darkened, being alienated from the life of God through the ignorance that is in them, because of the blindness of their heart" (Eph, 6:17, 18.) The natural darkness of the understanding, the ignorance of saving truth, is here plainly represented as an impediment in the way of salvation, while the innate blindness of the heart is declared to close it against the entrance of the word which giveth light and knowledge.

It is unnecessary to multiply proofs in a matter so plain, If knowledge were not necessary, all instruction in the truth would be merely waste of time and talents. As it is, "how shall they call on Him in whom they have not believed? and how shall they believe in Him of whom they have not heard?" (Rom, 10:14.) As we cannot believe what we do not know, God mercifully gives "knowledge of salvation unto His people by the remission of their sins." (Luke 1:77.)

The proper object of faith is the whole truth of God as given by revelation in the Holy Scriptures. The whole truth is therefore also the proper object of knowledge as an element of that faith. The Christian strives to "grow in grace and in the knowledge of our Lord and Savior Jesus Christ," that his faith may increase. He therefore willingly hears the Word of God and learns it, searching the Scriptures daily. But manifestly the whole contents of the Bible can be fully known by comparatively but few, while a large proportion of Christians remain in ignorance of many truths which are profitable for instruction. The knowledge of all is not essential to faith. The Scriptures therefore represent those truths which are indispensable to faith, as pre-eminently the object of knowledge. Thus St Paul ardently desires that the disciples' "hearts might be comforted, being knit together in love, and unto all riches of the full assurance of understanding; to the acknowledgment of the mystery of God, and of the Father, and of Christ, in whom are hid all the treasures of wisdom and knowledge." (Col. 2:2, 3.) And, again, he prays God to grant to His people "to know the love of Christ which passeth knowledge, that they might be filled with all the fullness of God." (Eph. 3:19.) Standing out prominently among the blessed truths revealed to man are those concerning the grace of God in our adorable Savior the redemption through His blood, and the promise of everlasting life in His dear name. While faith may exist without the knowledge of some portions of the Bible-truth, it cannot exist without the knowledge of such cardinal portions as these. We must know the truth forming the foundation of our salvation in order to have faith, and we exercise faith only so far as our knowledge extends.

But necessary as knowledge is, it is not the only element of faith, nor is it the chief. The error of identifying this one element with that of which it is a constituent part is ruinous to souls. Not all the learning of earth can secure a sinner's pardon, even though that learning embraced the whole Bible within its scope. Knowledge alone avails nothing on the judgment-day. Of it, considered as separated from the other elements of faith, the apostle asserts that it "puffeth up." (1 Cor. 8:1.) It profits no more for salvation than any other possession acquirable by natural means. The knowledge to which the Scriptures ascribe eternal life, it must be observed, is not that which may abide in the soul in harmony with the rejection of the truth known. When it is said that to know Christ is life eternal, the term knowledge is used synecdochically, one of the constituents of faith being placed for the whole. This is plain from the fact, that mere knowledge, exclusively of assent and confidence, merely "puffeth up," and has no saving power. The faith that saves implies something more.

2. It involves assent to that which is known. There are many who obtain a knowledge of divine truths without becoming believers. Some neglect them with indifference, some reject them with scorn. Faith implies that what is known is also approved.

In these last times especially, when the gates of hell are gathering all their strength to prevail against the Church, and philosophy and science are making their boldest and most desperate assaults upon the Book of God, all who would be saved from the wrath to come should be mindful of the fact, that the abandonment of truth which the Holy Spirit has revealed is the abandonment of faith. When the soul no longer clings to the Word of the Lord as absolute authority, and ceases to hold its testimony as a sufficient ground of assurance over against the adverse pretensions of human wisdom and human fancy, it is a mere delusion to suppose that it still retains the faith that saves. When God speaks, His servants hear. Not on condition that what He says is in coincidence with our reason or our taste, or seems to us adapted to the great end of man's salvation, is His Word received by the believer with reverence and held fast as a treasure. Faith regards it as supreme authority. "For this cause also thank we God without ceasing," says St. Paul, "because when ye received the word of God which ye heard of me, ye received it not as the word of man, but, as it is in truth, the word of God, which effectually worketh also in you that believe." (1 Thess. 2:14.)

There can be no true faith where the supremacy of God's Word is not recognized, and where assent is not given to every declaration as of divine authority, to which the whole soul must be in subjection. The believer stands in awe of the great King's words, "bringing into captivity every thought to the obedience of Christ." (2 Cor. 10:5.) Where one word of the Lord, being known as such, is rejected, faith cannot exist; because the authority on which all rests is repudiated. If the testimony of God is not regarded as sufficient ground for receiving that which it supports, His Word is not believed even when our convictions coincide with its statements, as these convictions must, in that case, be based upon some other evidence. But faith is the assurance of things not seen, on the ground of the witness of the Spirit given in the

Scriptures. Without assenting to the truth of this Word no saving faith could exist in the soul, as the very foundation of its confidence would be wanting; but where this foundation is recognized, there is not mere uncertain and vacillating opinion regarding its contents, but assent to eternal truth.

Nor is this approval confined to the general statements of Scripture: it embraces the particular declarations and the special application of those which are general. "Thou believest that there is one God; thou doest well: the devils also believe and tremble." (James 2:19.) Assenting to Biblical statements in a general way, while the heart is too little concerned about their import to effect a distinct recognition of what they imply, just as we give a general assent to historical statements about which we are indifferent and which have been but superficially viewed, is by no means all that is requisite. An assent by implication is futile; and no reasonable person would claim that the whole could be approved when there is not even the profession of assent to the parts composing it. To approve the proposition that God is just and merciful, and that He has sent His Son to satisfy the demands of justice and give mercy free scope in the salvation of the sinner, and yet to withhold assent to the implied proposition that He is just and merciful towards me and has sent His Son that might not perish, but have everlasting life, is contradictory and nugatory. The assent must be special. Thus we have it in the words of St. Paul: "This is a faithful saying, and worthy of all acceptation, that Christ Jesus came into the world to save sinners; of whom I am chief." (1 Tim. 1:15.) The object of faith is presented upon the authority of God; and faith cannot, in the nature of the case, have any existence where this object is not sanctioned by the judgment, on the ground of that divine authority. And yet this approval of the truth known does not, without still another element, constitute saving faith.

3. The other element necessary is confidence, which is, indeed, the most important of all. Faith is not merely the intellectual activity of knowing and approving, but includes also the exercise of the will and heart in reference to that which is known and approved. "Our opponents," says the Apology of the Augsburg Confession, "suppose this to be faith, that I know or have heard the history of Christ, and therefore teach that I can believe even though I live in mortal sin. Hence they know and say nothing of the true Christian

faith, of which Paul everywhere speaks, that we become righteous before God through faith. For those whom God accounts holy and righteous do not live in mortal sins. The faith which renders us just before God does not consist simply in the knowledge of the history concerning Christ's birth, sufferings, etc., which the devils also know; but in the certainty, or the certain strong confidence in the heart, by which, with all my heart, I hold as certain and true the assurance of God, which offers to me, without my merit, forgiveness of sin, grace, and full salvation through the Mediator Christ. And that no one may presume that it is merely a knowledge of the historical narratives, I add this, that faith consists in embracing this treasure with all my heart; that it is not my own deed, not a gift of my own bestowing, not a work of my own accomplishing, but a complete trust of the heart, with strong consolation, in the truth that God bestows gifts upon us, not we upon Him, and that He showers upon us the whole treasure of grace in Christ." (II., 48.) The true believer not only knows the truth in Jesus and assents to it intellectually, but also earnestly desires and seeks the mercy of God in Christ, and embraces the offer of pardon, freely made, as his daily consolation and joy, confiding in the word and promise of God, as directed to him personally and assuring him of eternal life through the Redeemer's blood.

That such confidence is an essential element of justifying faith, according to the Scriptures, must be clear to all candid minds from the following testimony:

First, faith is the reception of the Savior, the apprehension of Him with His infinite merits. This reception cannot take place by a mere intellectual assent, without an activity of the will, no more than an earthly object can be embraced by the mere knowledge of its existence without a volition. "As many as received Him, to them gave He power to become the sons of God, even to them that believe on His name." (John 1:12.) Here receiving Jesus is explained as identical with believing in Him. In John 17:8, the reception of the Savior's words is, in the same way, represented as identical with believing in Him. In John 17:8, the reception of the Savior's words is, in the same way, represented as identical with believing them: "I have given unto them the words which Thou gavest Me; and they have received them, and have known surely that I came out from Thee, and they have believed that Thou didst send Me." Of the same import are the words of the apostle: "That the blessing of Abraham might come on the Gentiles through Jesus Christ, that we might receive the promise of the Spirit through faith" (Gal. 3:14); and many of a similar character. All of these imply that faith is something more than a mere activity of the intellect, since receiving an object is manifestly a distinct operation, which cannot be considered identical with knowing it, or assenting to a proposition respecting it; and the reception and retention by the soul of the object of faith is just what confidence implies, as spiritual grasping and holding fast.

This is, secondly, expressed still more emphatically in the passages which ascribe to faith the appropriation of the benefits inhering in the object received. "I am crucified with Christ, nevertheless I live; yet not I, but Christ liveth in me: and the life which I now live in the flesh I live by the faith of the Son of God, who loved me and gave Himself for me." (Gal. 2:20.) "For ye are all the children of God by faith in Christ Jesus." (Gal 3:26.) Believing in Christ is holding Him fast in the soul, so as to enjoy all that He is and all that He has.

And this confidence, finally, is expressly declared to be an element of faith when it is said: "Let us draw near with a true heart in full assurance of faith" (Heb. 10:22); and, "Abraham staggered not at the promise of God through unbelief; but was strong in faith, giving glory to God, and being fully persuaded that what He had promised He was able also to perform." (Rom. 4:20, 21.) The full assurance and firm persuasion signify just what the word confidence is designed to express. If there should be any remaining doubt it must certainly be dispelled by passages such as these: "Such trust have we through Christ to Godward" (2 Cor. 3:4); "in whom we have boldness and access with confidence by the faith of Him" (Eph. 3:12); "and this is the confidence that we have in Him, that, if we ask anything according to His will, He heareth us." (1 John 5).

Saving faith is therefore not what many, who confound the Scriptural sense of the word with its ordinary acceptation in popular usage with reference to temporal things, conceive it to be. When it is understood as signifying merely an intellectual operation, which is performed by natural power, as simply a human conviction resting upon satisfactory evidence, which one who at heart rejects Christ may possess as well as one who most cordially embraces Him, it is no wonder that its justifying power is denied, and that the doctrine of justification by faith seems dangerous. "Faith is the substance of things hoped for, the evidence of things not seen." (Heb. 11:1.) "Whosoever believeth that Jesus is the Christ is born of God"; and "whatsoever is born of God overcometh the world: and this is the victory that overcometh the world, even our faith." (1 John 5:4.) It embraces the Savior and appropriates His merits, at the same time that it knows the truth and assents to it. It cannot exist without knowledge of its object, nor without the intellect's approval of the truth; but its chief characteristic is the strong confidence which will not let the Savior go, and which clings to Him, as presented to the soul by the Word of truth, in spite of the opposition of the devil and of the world and of the flesh. "For only faith in the heart keeps the promises of God in view, and faith alone is the assurance which renders the heart certain that God is gracious and that Christ has not died in vain. And this faith alone overcomes the terrors of death and of sin; for he that wavers, or doubts whether his sins are forgiven, has no confidence in God and despairs of Christ, deeming his sins greater and mightier than the death and blood of Christ." (Apology, III. 27, 28.)

Section 5.

HOW FAITH JUSTIFIES.

The doctrine of Justification by faith, clear and consistent as it is in itself, is often rendered an enigma by the misrepresentations of its opponents. Some misconceive, and some perhaps willfully pervert, the truth in regard to the manner in which faith is said to justify the sinner; and upon the basis of such misconception the doctrine seems singularly illogical and unsatisfactory. We shall endeavor, in this section, to obviate the difficulties which may appear to surround the truth on account of misapprehensions respecting the functions of faith in the work of justification.

It is not strange that when the Scriptural doctrine is understood as resting on the assumption of the meritoriousness of faith as a human activity, the difference between it and the doctrine which ascribes justification to good works is not easily discerned. But the Scriptural doctrine involves no such assumption. Faith does not justify as being a good work. It is not meritorious, and if it were, its merit could not satisfy the requirements of justice. It is not meritorious, because it is the gift of God's grace, upon which it would be absurd to base a claim against the bountiful Giver. It could not justify as a meritorious work, even if it were admitted to be such, because all human work is imperfect, and even perfection in holiness could not atone for past sins. When faith is spoken of as justifying, it is not viewed at all as a work performed, but rather as a means used. Therefore the Lutheran Church says in her Confession that "faith does not render us just and righteous before God because it is our work, but only because it accepts the grace promised and proffered as a free gift without merit." The opinion that faith is a meritorious act of man, and that God, in consideration of such merit, justifies the sinner, is in conflict with the truth that man is justified by grace through Christ Jesus; and its adoption into the Lutheran system would render this a confused mass of contradictions. But this opinion is Romish, not Evangelical, and will not harmonize with the doctrine of Scripture, which can recognize no merit before God in any human performance. The sinner is justified by faith, not on account of it.

Neither is it the teaching of Scripture and of the Church that faith justifies so far forth as it implies a change of heart, and is thus sanctification in its germ. Justification by faith is not justification by the holiness of which it is the root, and which it might be conceived as potentially possessing. It is undoubtedly true that the existence of faith implies the co-existence in the heart of incipient sanctification. It is inconceivable that there could be a living trust in Jesus while the soul which trusts disregards His holy will and resists His Spirit of holiness. "Whosoever believeth that Jesus is the Christ, is born of God." (1 John 5:1.) We "cannot by our own reason or other natural powers believe in or come to Jesus Christ." Faith is not a product of human exertion; it cannot originate in man's own will. "For by grace are ye saved through faith; and that not of yourselves: it is the gift of God." (Eph. 2:8.) "No man can come unto Me, except it were given unto him of My Father." (John 6:65.) Faith can exist only as the result of the Holy Spirit's operation in the heart through His appointed means. But the Holy Spirit, whose will is our sanctification, as well as our justification, does not confine His work within us to the production of faith. "The fruit of the Spirit is love, joy, peace, long-suffering, gentleness, goodness, faith, meekness, temperance: against such there is no law. And they that are Christ's have crucified the flesh with the affections and lusts." (Gal 5:22-24.) The work of sanctification is begun just as soon as the Holy Spirit enters the heart, and it exists therefore in its incipiency as soon as living faith is wrought. The knowledge of sin, and sense of misery, and desire for relief must precede the appropriation of comfort; and the heart which does not obstinately resist the grace enabling it to embrace the comfort, possesses the grace enabling it to hate the sin which entailed the misery. All things become new when we believe in Christ. "The faith by which each one believes that Christ is given for him personally, alone receives forgiveness of sin for Christ's sake, and renders us just and righteous before God. And because this exists where there is true penitence, and supports us in the terrors of sin and death, we are born anew by it. By faith the Holy Spirit enters our hearts and renews us, so that we are able to keep the divine law, truly to love and fear God, firmly to trust that Christ is given to us, and cheerfully to resign ourselves to the will of God, even in the midst of death." (Apology, 2. 45)

A faith that is not thus connected with holiness is the dead faith of which St. James speaks, and which is just as little justifying as it is sanctifying. To ascribe justification to such a lifeless thing betrays an utter want of understanding in spiritual matters, and to impute such blindness and stupidity to the great Reformer and his brethren in the faith of Jesus is foully slanderous. "It is indisputable that on our part the correct doctrine is taught concerning good works. And we add that it is impossible that true faith, which comforts the heart and embraces forgiveness of sins, should exist without the love of God." (Ap. 2. 20.)

But while the truth is undeniable that a living faith is never sundered from the sanctifying influences of the Spirit who dwells in the hearts of believers, it is equally certain that the holy affections which accompany it are neither the ground nor the means of justification. A grosser misunderstanding of the precious doctrine which we teach can scarcely be conceived than that which, when faith is mentioned, assumes that works are meant. It overthrows the very foundation of our salvation, which is Christ, to substitute the latter for the former. For if our holy emotions or performances effect our acceptance with God, then has Christ become to us of none effect. What need have we for a Savior if we can save ourselves? Why speak any longer of the merits of Christ as the ground of our hope, if that ground is the sanctification which we ourselves possess?

Nor does it materially change the question to remind us that the necessity of faith is not denied, but that it is only viewed in connection with its fruits, by those who would have the holiness resulting from it considered the justifying element. For in this way faith would become the means of laying the foundation of righteousness in ourselves, instead of being the means of bringing us into a living relation with the foundation which is laid. Christ is thus set aside to make room for a sinner whose saintliness is supposed to need no justification. If, in such a doctrine, Christ is recognized at all, it can be only as a medium through whom we are brought to heaven without needing an atonement, since we can render satisfaction ourselves. This is a fatal perversion of the truth. Faith justifies in no such sense. As it is not itself a holy sentiment on account of which all our unholiness is winked at and we are pronounced just, so it is not a source of holy affections which God declares sufficient to establish our claim to eternal bliss. Faith does produce holy fruits which are pleasing in God's sight. But never can these fruits atone for the sin which is upon us, or avert the wrath of God under which it has brought us. Without Christ we are inevitably lost. "Other foundation can no man lay than that is laid, which is Jesus Christ." Faith can in itself no more be the foundation than charity. A believer can no more be saved by holiness than an unbeliever, just as a genuine dime will no more buy a palace than a spurious one. Faith is the means to embrace Christ, that we may be saved through Him; not a means of enabling us to dispense with Him, and still to be saved. The theory that it saves the sinner so far forth as it sanctifies, or because it sanctifies, is a Romish figment, which only those Protestant sects have adopted who have fallen away from the sound and solacing doctrines of the Bible as revived in the glorious Reformation. The faith which saves is, beyond all controversy, the faith which works by love, as it is a living faith; but it saves only because it appropriates the Savior, in no sense because it works by love.

Saving faith has a two-fold energy. It is both receptive and operative. It has two hands, one of which is extended towards the Lamb of God who became a sacrifice for us, while the other ministers to the wants of the brethren. It appropriates the redemption, and, in the strength of the grace which it appropriates, it dispenses blessings in good works. It clings to Jesus for the saving of the soul, and works by love for the welfare of our race, that God may be glorified in all. The precious doctrine of Justification by faith cannot be held in its purity or experienced in its preciousness where this two-fold energy is not recognized, and where the effect of each is not viewed without confounding it with that of the other.

Faith receives the Savior with all His fullness of grace. "As many as received Him, to them gave He power to become the sons of God, even to them that believe on His name." (John 1:12.) It is not by holy affections which beseem the children of God that we are made such children: we become such by the reception in faith of the only begotten Son, in whom the Father is well-pleased. Receiving Him is identical with believing in Him. Therefore the apostle, after telling the Colossians that he joyed in their steadfastness of faith in Christ, tells them: "As ye have therefore received Christ Jesus the Lord, so walk ye in Him, rooted and built up in Him, and established in the faith." (Col. 2:6, 7.) By faith they had received Christ, and it behooved them to order their conversation accordingly, that they might walk worthy of Him. And those who thus embrace Him become recipients of His merits unto salvation. "To Him give all the prophets witness, that through His name whosoever believes in Him shall receive remission of sin." (Acts 10:43.) The faith which receives Him receives all that He has secured for us, having righteousness not in that which it is, but in that which it holds. "That no man is justified by the law in the sight of God, it is evident; for, The just shall live by faith. And the law is not of faith; but, The man that does them shall live in them. Christ hath redeemed us from the curse of the law, being made a curse for us; for it is written, Cursed is every one that hangs on a tree; that the blessings of Abraham might come on the Gentiles through Jesus Christ, that we might receive the promise of the Spirit through faith." (Gal. 3:11-14.) It is because of this receptive energy of faith that St. Paul declares: "To him that works not, but believes on Him that justifies the ungodly, his faith is counted for righteousness." (Rom. 4:5.) Faith avails unto justification, not because of any intrinsic virtue which it has in itself, but because of the merit which it holds by embracing Christ. It receives the Savior, and therefore has Him and all that He has.

From this receptive power of faith its operative power, as directed towards man, is clearly distinguishable. The reception of Christ is the condition of all holiness and good works. It gives the necessary strength and furnishes the requisite motives; "for we are His workmanship, created in Christ Jesus unto good works, which God hath before ordained that we should walk in them." (Eph. 2:10.) But never is the love which it produces, and through which it works, laid down in the Scriptures as the justifying power or the justifying medium. Faith justifies not because it is operative in scattering blessings through love upon our fellow-men, but only and solely because it receives Christ with all His grace and merits unto salvation.

Section 6.

DEGREES IN FAITH, BUT NOT IN JUSTIFICATION.

The faith which justifies admits of degrees. In some it is comprehensive, in others it is narrow; in some it is strong, in others it is weak. It grows, and conditions the Christian's growth. Step by step we approach the stature of the perfect man. All have reason to pray with the apostles: "Lord, increase our faith." (Luke 17:5.) But as this increase is slower in some, more rapid in others, its degrees are manifold.

Of faith in its strength we have an illustrious example in Abraham, "who against hope believed in hope, that he might become the father of many nations, according to that which was spoken, So shall thy seed be. And being not weak in faith, he considered not his own body now dead, when he was about a hundred years old, neither yet the deadness of Sarah's womb; he staggered not at the promise of God through unbelief, but was strong in faith, giving glory to God." (Rom. 4:19-20.) Of faith in its weakness an illustration is presented in the man who entreated the Lord to deliver his son from the "dumb spirit" by which he was tormented. He said to Jesus: "If thou canst do anything, have compassion on us and help us. Jesus said unto him, If thou canst believe, all things are possible to him that believes. And straightway the father of the child cried out, and said with tears, Lord, I believe: help Thou mine unbelief." (Mark 9:22-24.) The former had strong confidence that permitted no doubt to vex his soul; the latter trusted so feebly that a rigorous judge might construe his faith into unbelief. Both were believers, but they had faith in strikingly different degrees.

The distinction between a strong and a weak faith is frequently suggested in the Scriptures, and duties are enjoined upon Christians which rest upon the fact of such distinction. Thus the apostle exhorts: "Him that is weak in the faith receive ye, but not to doubtful disputations." (Rom. 14:1.) And having explained and enforced the duty, he sums up by saying: "We then that are strong ought to bear the infirmities of the weak, and not to please ourselves." (Rom. 15:1.) The assumption that all believers possess faith in the same stage of development is utterly inconsistent with such declarations.

The fact that faith is capable of growth implies that it does not always exist in the same degree. It is the will of God that we should increase "till we all come, in the unity of the faith and the knowledge of the Son of God, unto a perfect man, unto the measure of the stature of the fullness of Christ: that we henceforth be no more children, tossed to and fro, and carried about with every wind of doctrine, by the sleight of men and cunning craftiness, whereby they lay in wait to deceive." (Eph. 4:13, 14.) That Christians will make progress is accordingly presupposed by the apostle when he writes: "We are come as far as to you also in preaching the Gospel of Christ: not boasting of things without our measure, that is, of other men's labors; but having hope, when your faith is increased, that we shall be enlarged by you according to our rule abundantly." (2 Cor. 10:14, 15.)

The increase of faith is dependent upon the increase of the elements which constitute it. Faith grows on the condition that the field of our knowledge of its proper object is enlarged, that our assent attains a correspondingly wider range, and that our confidence in that which is known and approved as divine is strengthened. Not every believer has precisely the same degree of knowledge and of confidence.

We cannot exercise intelligent faith in more than we know, and therefore increase in knowledge is urged upon us as a pre-requisite to the increase of faith. Thus St. Paul says: "For this cause we also, since the day we heard it, do not cease to pray for you, and to desire that ye might be filled with the knowledge of His will in all wisdom and spiritual understanding; that ye might walk worthy of the Lord unto all pleasing, being fruitful in every good work, and increasing in the knowledge of God." (Col. 1:9, 10.) Thus also St. Peter exhorts: "Ye therefore, beloved, seeing ye know these things before, beware lest ye also, being led away with the error of the wicked, fall from your own steadfastness. But grow in grace, and in the knowledge of your Lord and Savior Jesus Christ." (2 Peter 3:17, 18.) It is so manifest as scarcely to need mentioning, that the enlargement of the sphere of our knowledge does not involve of necessity the increase of faith, since we may withhold our assent and confidence from that which has been learned and which should be believed. But while we may know the truth without embracing it by faith, we cannot thus embrace it without knowing it. Knowledge avails nothing without faith; but, having faith, the increase of knowledge in revealed truth constitutes an increase of faith in its volume, and contributes to its increase in power. The degree of our faith must manifestly, in its extent, be commensurate with the degree of our knowledge of that to which faith clings and without which it can have no existence, although the degree of our confidence is not always as the degree of our knowledge.

As mere knowledge, indispensable as it is to faith, does not alone constitute it, and as an individual may be well informed in the domain of divine truth without actually appropriating it, the increase of faith depends upon something more than the enlargement of our knowledge. In one respect it might, indeed, be said that assent is incapable of degrees. As this is an intellectual act, into which the will does not enter, as one of the factors, it might be claimed that it absolutely takes place, or it does not take place at all, and that when assent is wanting there is absolutely no faith. In regard to assent in general it is to be observed, however, that it will be proportioned to the strength of the evidence, and that we assent upon probabilities as well as upon certainties, only in different ways; that is, assent has different degrees. And in regard to the special assent which is an element of saving faith, it must not be overlooked that that which seems to preclude all degrees does not lie in its nature, but in the nature of the object. Assent may be but partial when the object is but partially admissible, or it may be more or less strong, according as that object seems more or less probable. But divine truth is certain, and cannot be more so or less so; and if, in this domain, the assent is but partial, because the Word of God is deemed only partly true, or but feeble, because that Word seems only probable, the special assent implied in faith is not given at all, because the object is not received at all as infallible truth. It is then approved only on human grounds, and this implies the rejection of the whole ground upon which it rests. This is absolutely inconsistent with faith, according to St. Paul's words: "For this cause also thank we God without ceasing, because, when ye received the word of God which ye heard of us, ye received it not as the word of men, but, as it is in truth, the word of God, which effectually worketh in you also that believe." (2 Thess. 2:13.) In this regard the question respecting which there are degrees in the assent would be, whether that which is claimed to be so is the word of the Lord. But there is a respect, in which assent increases constantly. It keeps pace with knowledge in all the growth of the latter: its domain becomes ever wider. To know a truth of revelation and not to assent to it, is unbelief Knowledge and assent go hand in hand in the believer, and faith increases as its possessions become larger through the enlargement of its territory.

But growth in faith also implies growth in the vigor with which its proper object is held fast. It must increase as well intensively as extensively. Not only must knowledge increase and assent be given to all that is known as God's word, but this must be adhered to with ever-increasing tenacity. Confidence, which is the chief element in faith, and constitutes its distinctive character as saving faith, must become constantly stronger. It endures trials, and becomes ever more vigorous by the endurance. The Christian is "kept by the power of God through faith unto salvation, ready to be revealed in the last time; wherein ye greatly rejoice, though now for a season, if need be, ye are in heaviness through manifold temptations; that the trial of your faith, being much more precious than of gold that perisheth, though it be tried by fire, might be found unto praise and honor and glory at the appearing of Jesus Christ." (2 Peter 1:5-7.) The difference between a faith that clings, in weal and wo, through storm and sunshine, to the promises of God, and a faith that trembles at every danger and shrinks from every conflict, though it still in feebleness clasps the Savior, is manifest; and examples of both are mentioned in Scripture and met with frequency in our intercourse with men. Those who have not observed a difference of degree in the power of faith as exhibited in different persons, must have walked among Christians with their eyes closed.

With the fact clearly before us that there are different degrees of faith, it is of the utmost importance for our own peace of conscience, and for the exercise of justice and charity to others, that we be fully assured of the justifying power of faith, even where it lacks that high degree of advancement which characterizes it in the Christian hero. Faith that embraces Christ as the Savior justifies in any of its degrees; and the justification which it secures is not graduated according to the degree of the faith which secures it.

That which is requisite to justification is faith, not a certain definite degree of faith. It is unquestionable that this is the means by which the merits of Christ are embraced and appropriated. But frequently as the necessity of faith is declared and its justifying power is proclaimed, there is not a single passage which requires a certain stage in its development to be attained as a condition of its efficacy. It must embrace the Savior as offered in the Word of truth; for there is no other name than that of Jesus by which the soul can be saved. It must, in other words, have Him for its object, in whom alone there is justification. But whether it clings to Him firmly or feebly, so long as it continues to cling to Him, is not essential in the sphere of justification, however important it, is in the domain of sanctification. "He that believes shall be saved," whether his faith be strong or weak. The attainment of strength must be the Christian's persistent aim; for the weak are always in more danger of falling away than the strong, and thus of failing at last to reach the end of their faith, which is the salvation of the soul; and the strong can accomplish more for the glory of God, which is the end of our being, and have a prospect of higher prizes in the distribution of gracious rewards to the saved in the kingdom of glory. "The just shall live by faith"; but "he that endures to the end shall be saved" (Mat. 10:22); and "they that be wise shall shine as the brightness of the firmament, and they that turn many to righteousness, as the stars for ever and ever." (Dan. 12:3, comp. 1 Cor. 15:41, 42.) It is therefore by no means indifferent whether we grow and abound more and more or not. But it is just as little a matter of indifference whether we represent our salvation as dependent upon the degree of our growth or not. It is a fearful thing to discourage tremulous souls, who pursue the path of faith amid untold difficulties already, by telling them that their weakness insures their damnation. Despair may be the result of such harshness, which conflicts at once with truth and mercy; and the soul that is too severely judged, and the soul which judges too severely, are both endangered. "Him that is weak in the faith receive ye," (Rom. 14:1,) as it is said of our Lord: "A bruised reed shall He not break, and the smoking flax shall He not quench." (Is. 62:3.)

Indeed, the figment that a certain degree of faith, not faith itself, secures justification, is in conflict with the great central truth of Christianity, and saps its very foundation. For if the faith which appropriates Christ does not save because it is weak, then the salvation is not found in Christ, but in the faith. Man in this way would become his own Savior. The redemption in Christ would no longer be its ground. Faith would justify, not because it appropriates the justifying merits of Jesus, but because it has an intrinsic justifying virtue. We meet thus the old papistic foe with a new face. It is salvation by creature merit, justification through sanctification. It declares that Christ, whom faith embraces, avails nothing; that which alone is of avail is the moral strength which the soul possesses. It transforms the precious doctrine of justification through the merits of Christ, apprehended by faith, into the disconsolate fiction of justification through the merits of faith. The latter is viewed as a meritorious work under the law, and the words of the apostle are as well applicable to this as to any other work: "Christ is become of no effect unto you, whosoever of you are justified by the law; ye are fallen from grace." (Gal 5:4.)

It would avail nothing to reply that no merit is ascribed to faith by those who advocate the theory of justification only by a certain degree of faith, inasmuch as they mean nothing more than this, that only when such degree is attained has it power to appropriate the salvation in Christ. This is simply shirking the question. Faith which does not apprehend Christ in His Word certainly does not save: it is not saving faith. About this there can be no controversy. But saving faith may be strong or weak; the faith which does embrace Christ admits of different degrees; and those who maintain that a weak faith, though it be right in kind, does not justify because it is insufficient in degree, undoubtedly teach that faith may be sufficient to embrace Christ without being sufficient to justify; and this just as undeniably involves the error that not the merits of Christ, but the merits of faith, are the ground of justification. Let not souls be deprived of the rich comfort which lies in the truth that, while they cling to the Lamb of God which taketh away the sins of the world, they are not under condemnation, but are justified, notwithstanding all their weaknesses. Imperfection attaches to everything human, and faith is not exempt from it; for although it is the work and gift of God, it is exercised by man and partakes of human infirmity. To pronounce salvation impossible while this infirmity attaches to our faith, is to deprive us of all hope; and to declare a certain degree of strength indispensable in the faith which embraces Christ, to render it justifying, is to dishearten the weak tremblers, who, of all others, need encouragement most. Just as decidedly must we reject the error of those who maintain that there are degrees of justification corresponding to the degrees of faith.

The believer grows in the fullness of his knowledge and in the firmness of his grasp of the truth; he grows in the joyous consciousness of his rich possessions in Christ: but justification, being an act of God, is perfect and complete at once, and it is the sinner's personal possession as soon as he has the faith which appropriates it. It is incapable of division into parts or degrees in itself, and it is embraced in its entirety, not partially and gradually, if embraced at all. The theory of the Romish Church, which, in its essential features, has lately been adopted and advocated with great zeal by a prominent Protestant theologian in Germany, and which he has labored hard to bring into coincidence with the pure Lutheran faith, finds not the least countenance in the Bible. It can be entertained only by those who confound the distinct offices of the Law and the Gospel, and who, in consequence of such confusion, are incapable of distinguishing between justification and sanctification.

If we do not wrest the Scriptures, but accept their statements in their plain import, we cannot for a moment remain in doubt whether justification is at once perfect. The blood of Jesus Christ His Son cleanses us from all sin. If we say that we have no sin, we deceive ourselves, and the truth is not in us. If we confess our sins, He is faithful and just to forgive us our sins, and to cleanse us from all unrighteousness." (1 John 1:7-9.) In this passage the Holy Spirit twice declares that by the grace of God in Christ we are delivered from the curse of all sin and unrighteousness, not only of a portion. The same precious truth is also expressed in Romans 8:1: "There is now no condemnation to them which are in Christ Jesus." If there were any sins remaining from which the blood of Jesus has not cleansed the believer, there must also be condemnation remaining upon him. We cannot be free from the inevitable effect without being free from the cause. Of the same import are the words in Hebrews 10:14: "For by one offering He hath perfected forever them that are sanctified." It would overthrow the whole foundation of our faith to pervert this into the declaration, that the sacrifice of Christ perfects those who have been previously perfected in holiness; whilst it would, at the same time, involve a palpable absurdity. For there is no need for perfecting those who are perfected already, and there is no need for the sacrifice of Christ if souls can be perfected prior to any influences exerted upon them by it. Such an interpretation would leave us a Christianity without Christ, and thus without grace and truth and life. The expression, "them that are sanctified," evidently means them that are "in Christ Jesus, who of God is made unto us wisdom and righteousness and sanctification and redemption"; in other words, "them that believe on His name." The offering of Christ perfects the work of salvation, and those who embrace Christ are perfected in Him: if they appropriate Him at all they have a perfect Savior. "You, being dead in your sins and the uncircumcision of your flesh, hath He quickened together with Him, having forgiven you all trespasses; blotting out the handwriting of ordinances that was against us, which was contrary to us, and took it out of the way, nailing it to His cross." (Col, 2:13, 14.) It would seem impossible to read such passages without prejudice and still find them consistent with the notion, that the believing sinner's justification is imperfect and approaches its goal only gradually. This Romish figment is totally at variance with the analogy of faith, and can by no art of errorists be brought into harmony with it.

We find it difficult to conceive how, without renouncing truths which are fundamental in Christianity, thoughtful men can assume that the sinner, when he has faith in Christ, is partially in grace and partially not. It cannot be presumed that the soul is thought of as divided into parts, some of which are accepted of God, while others are not. The idea is too extravagant to be imputed to persons of intelligence. And it would be no less preposterous to imagine that either the soul or the body is an heir of heaven, while one or the other is not: we would not impute such a fancy to the advocates of gradual justification. The object of grace must be the whole man, and the assumption of such advocates must be that the grace of God is bestowed upon the sinner but only partially. But that would imply that divine grace is imperfect. The believing soul receives what is given, and if it has not complete forgiveness of sins and perfect righteousness in Christ, it is because these were not bestowed in their completeness and perfection. If full grace unto justification and salvation be offered, the feebleness with which the sinner apprehends it cannot detract from its fullness, no more than holding a jewel with a feeble grasp renders it imperfect. There is more danger of losing it when it is feebly held; but it is held entire while it is held at all.

But if God bestows His merits partially, it must be either because the redemption through Christ is incomplete, so that the justice of God would forbid the bestowal of full pardon; or, because divine grace is not full and free, so that He does not desire the sinner's perfect justification. The former assumption is in direct conflict with numberless passages of Scripture, subverts the whole plan of salvation, and deprives the sinner of all his hopes. For if Christ only partially discharged our infinite debt, how shall the infinite balance ever be canceled? Christianity would then be as comfortless as the other religions of the world, and sinners would have nothing to expect but indignation and wrath forevermore. But if the latter assumption is adopted, our prospects are little brighter.

Any doctrine which robs the soul of its trust in the boundless mercy of its God, in which, conscious of its deserts, it alone can find solace, robs it of all joy and peace. The Scriptures do not so speak of our merciful Father in heaven, who spared not His own Son but freely gave Him up for us all, that He might have mercy on all. They do not ask us to lean upon the broken reed of our own righteousness. They do not point us to the filthy rags of our own holiness as a condition of receiving a wedding-garment through the mercy of God. "But God, who is rich in mercy, for His great love wherewith He loved us, even when we were dead in sins, hath quickened us together with Christ, (by grace ye are saved,) and hath raised us up together, and made us sit together in heavenly places in Christ Jesus, that in the ages to come He might show the exceeding riches of His grace, in His kindness toward us through Jesus Christ." (Eph. 2:4-7.) The redemption is perfect; the grace of God is infinite; God justifies the sinner perfectly. "This is the will of Him that sent Me, that everyone which seeth the Son, and believeth on Him, may have everlasting life." (John 5:4)

5

Its Effects

I N the great struggle of the XVI. Century called the Reformation, great prominence was given to the effect upon the soul of the reception of the doctrine of Justification by faith alone in the merits of Christ. It was plain then, as it is now, that the Roman theory, which makes the sinner's justification dependent upon his ceasing to be a sinner, could not quiet the troubled conscience, and that the designed effect of the Gospel could not in this way be produced. The experience of many earnest souls has proved that in humble reliance upon the merits of Christ joy and peace could be found. The argument from experience would be of no weight and value without the Word of God; for this must be received as true, let our experience be what it may. But our fathers did well and proceeded logically when they laid stress upon the blessed results which flow from the sound Biblical doctrine. They did not, as fanatics are wont to do, appeal to their experience against the literal sense of divine statements; but having shown what the Bible teaches, they found strong confirmation of the truth in the effect which its reception produced, as this effect was precisely that which the Gospel, according to its own statements, was designed to produce.

The doctrine of Justification, as taught by Luther and confessed by the Reformers, was not a philosophical speculation in which the heart had no concern. It had, under the direction of the Holy Spirit through the divine Word, been thoroughly experienced in the life, as it has been by millions since, and it has been found to give the rest to the soul which is vainly sought under any other doctrine. We devote this final chapter to an exhibition of those effects, because this furnishes a confirmation of the doctrine which has been presented, and also a refutation of the widespread opinion that mischievous results must ensue upon its adoption.

Section I.

IT GIVES THE CONSCIENCE PEACE.

"Therefore being justified by faith, we have peace with God through our Lord Jesus Christ." (Rom. 5:1)

There can be no peace without this; peace cannot fail to dwell in the soul that clings by faith to the Savior for justification. When there is a consciousness of sin the conscience is troubled. Sin entails misery. Justice is dreaded, as punishment is felt to be merited. "There is no peace, saith the Lord, unto the wicked." (Isaiah 47:22.) "Through fear of death they are all their lifetime subject to bondage." (Heb. 2:15.) Their conscience smites them and fills them with terror. "The wicked flee when no man pursueth." (Prov. 28:1.) Perceiving their guilt, they know death to be their due. It is utterly impossible to quiet the clamors of an awakened conscience as long as no refuge from the impending wrath is within reach. It avails nothing to form the resolution to cease from sin. Such resolutions are broken as soon as they are formed; they are felt to be futile, — because sin is felt in the soul even while amendment is meditated; they are clearly perceived to be useless as means to atone for iniquities already committed. The criminal, upon whom sentence of death has been passed, finds the determination to be guilty of no further murders a miserable comforter. There could be peace for him only in pardon. The terrors of a guilty conscience are not to be banished by thoughts of reforming. It is silly to think of this. No broken vessel is made whole again by the purpose not to break another, even if the purpose were executed. Those who would console the sinner with crudities like this, think lightly of divine justice and trifle with immortal souls. Even if they did

106

succeed in allaying the inner commotion for a season, it would only be to let it gather strength for more violent tossings. The first wave that rolls against the cobweb curb will wash it away. "They have healed also the hurt of the daughter of My people slightly, saying, Peace, peace; when there is no peace. Were they ashamed when they had committed abominations? nay, they were not at all ashamed, neither could they blush; therefore they shall fall among them that fall: at the time that I visit them they shall be cast down, saith the Lord. Thus saith the Lord, Stand ye in the ways, and see, and ask for the old paths, where is the good way, and walk therein, and ye shall find rest for your souls." (Jer. 6:14-16.)

Only when Christ is embraced by faith as the sure foundation that cannot fail us, is the conscience effectually quieted. There is then no condemnation; and although sin be still felt and deplored, the strong consolation abides that the Savior has died to put away sin, and that for His sake all is pardoned. "Who shall lay anything to the charge of God's elect? It is God that justifieth. Who is he that condemneth? It is Christ that died, yea rather, that is risen again, who is even at the right-hand of God, who also maketh intercession for us." (Rom. 8:33, 34.) When we have the full assurance of faith that the merits of our adored Surety and Substitute are imputed to us and all our sins are pardoned, we cannot fail to have the peace of God. "Ye who sometime were far off are made nigh by the blood of Christ; for He is our peace." (Eph. 2:14.) "The word which God sent unto the children of Israel, preaching peace by Jesus Christ: (He is Lord of all:) that word, I say, ye know." (Acts 10:36, 37.) Believers know assuredly that the Father is reconciled through the satisfaction rendered by His dear Son, and that therefore He will not lay their sins to their charge. "For I know the thoughts that I think towards you, saith the Lord, thoughts of peace and not of evil." (Jer. 29:11.) If we had to seek justification by our own works and merits we would be forever in torment, as these would never suffice. There can be no justification by the deeds of the law. But as the Lord is our righteousness, we heed the call which He gives us and find His word of promise sure: "Come unto Me, all ye that labor and are heavy laden; and I will give you rest." (Mat 11:28.) As surely as God cannot lie, so surely can we cling in confidence to the Savior of the world as our Savior, without a fear that His righteousness will fail us at the last. "The foundation of God standeth sure, having this seal, The Lord knoweth them that are His." (2 Tim. 2:19.) The Rock of Ages will not give way.

There are many, however, who, while they confess that the foundation stands sure, still doubt, and teach others to doubt, whether the sinner can ever be sure that he rests upon this foundation. The object of our faith is indubitably certain, they say, but the subject is not certain. Some even condemn those who teach that there can be any certainty of our justified state, and pronounce them heretics. This is the position of the Romish Church, and some others substantially agree with this great enemy of the doctrine of Justification by faith alone. Perceiving that a person may confess himself to be a believer and still show by his life that he is in a state of condemnation, they mingle the Law and the Gospel together, and demand a certain degree of holiness as requisite to justification. In this case it is evident that doubts must arise in the mind, whether a sufficient degree of progress in sanctification has been made to entitle the individual to the consolations of the Gospel, and peace cannot be found for the soul because of such doubts. The error lies in the false conception of the ground of our justification. If this were in any sense dependent upon our merit or preparation, doubts would be natural and necessary, and rest for the soul impossible; for doubt and unrest go hand in hand.

But those who accept the doctrine as the Spirit teaches it in the Bible, and as we have endeavored to present it, can see no foundation for human uncertainties and consequent fears in the Scriptural doctrine. The redemption of all is a fact. Its appropriation by faith is all that is requisite to enjoy it. Unbelief can have no peace, because it rejects the fact; faith cannot be deprived of peace, because it accepts the fact. The believer, so far as he actually has faith, has assurance: he accepts the Gospel statements as certain. When God makes the declaration, Thy sins are forgiven thee, we may deprive ourselves of the joy which the divine word is designed to give us, by affixing conditions of our own invention and then inferring that our sins are not forgiven because we have not fulfilled the self-imposed conditions. We destroy our peace and

108

rob ourselves of comfort most wantonly. But the fault lies not in the divine declaration, but in our refusal to accept that declaration just as it was given. We have no peace because we have no faith. The false doctrine, which forbids assurance on the ground of the gracious word of God, prevents assurance. There is nothing in the divine Word itself to prevent it. There are no demands made upon us which, on account of our sinfulness and weakness, forbid its existence in our souls. The word which declares us just is sure, resting upon the sure ground of the finished redemption; and if we believe it we have assurance and have a right "to have it. It is the Evil that suggests doubts by suggesting conditions which God has never made. He is a liar, and by his lies he seeks to introduce into our souls doubts of the truth of God's word, and thus to prevent assurance of our justification through faith, and peace with God. Men may doubt, but they have no reason to doubt; and those who teach that they ought to doubt, corrupt the Word of God and rob the souls of the peace which our Savior graciously secured. Those who believe the Bible doctrine of justification hold it to be a sin to doubt, and pray God to increase their faith, that Satan may not despoil them of their happy assurance. They know that although they are worthless, the blood of Jesus was shed for them and avails for their justification. They know that nothing is required but faith to render them heirs of heaven through Christ, and they therefore guard chiefly against the false doctrines which would undermine their faith, deprive them of their assurance, and rob them of the peace which they have in believing.

"Let us therefore give thanks unto God," says Luther, "that we are delivered from this monstrous doctrine of doubting, and can now assure ourselves that the Holy Ghost crieth, and bringeth forth in our hearts unspeak able groanings, and this is our anchor-hold and our foundation. The Gospel commandeth us to behold not our own good works, our own perfection; but God the Promiser, and Christ the Mediator. On the other hand, the pope commandeth us to look not unto God the Promiser, nor unto Christ our High Bishop, but unto our works and merits. Here, on the one side, doubting and desperation must needs follow; but, on the other side, assurance of God's favor and joy of the spirit. For we cleave unto God, who cannot lie. He saith:

Behold, I deliver my Son to death, that through His blood He may redeem thee from thy sins and from eternal, death. In this case I cannot doubt, unless I would utterly deny God. And this is the reason that our doctrine is most sure and certain, because it carrieth us out of ourselves, that we should not lean on our own strength, our own conscience, our own feeling, our own person, and our own works; but on that which is without us—that is to say, the promise and truth of God, which cannot deceive us. This the pope knoweth not, and therefore he wickedly imagineth that no man knoweth, be he never so just or so wise, whether he be worthy of love or of hatred. But if he be just and wise...he knoweth assuredly that he is beloved of God, or else he is neither just nor wise...The pope, therefore, with this devilish doctrine, whereby he commanded men to doubt of the favor of God towards them, took away God and all His promises out of the Church, buried all the benefits of Christ, and abolished the whole Gospel. These inconveniences do necessarily follow; for men do not lean on the promises of God, but on their own works and merits. Therefore they cannot be assured of the goodwill of God towards them, but must needs doubt thereof, and so at length despair. No man can understand what God's will is, and what pleaseth Him, but in His good Word. This Word assureth us that God cast away all the anger and displeasure which He had conceived against us, when He gave His only-begotten Son for our sins. Wherefore, let us wholly abandon this devilish doubting, wherewith the whole papacy was poisoned, and let us be fully assured that God is merciful unto us."

The peace which we feel in believing must not be made the ground or condition of our justification. It would seem superfluous to add this caution against a procedure that is so absurd, were it not that many are actually guilty of the strange absurdity, and thus rob themselves of all peace by leaving it without a foundation. They saw off the limb upon which they sit. Supposing themselves justified because they have peace, and considering this the only satisfactory reason for thinking themselves justified at all, they set aside the only evidence upon which the soul can have assurance—namely, that of the Word— and trust in effects, which are not uniform, and the testimony of which is therefore precarious.

If a person has faith in Christ, he is justified, and, knowing himself to be justified, he has peace and joy. But if this peace and this joy are necessary before he can know himself to be justified, whence is he to derive them? If we have peace upon any other ground than that of the redemption through Christ and the forgiveness of sin for His sake as conveyed to us in the word of the Gospel, we have a false peace, which proves nothing but that we have been deceiving ourselves. If we have peace upon this only true ground of the redemption appropriated by faith, this peace is, in our consciousness, a result of our assurance that we are justified, not a ground upon which that assurance rests. The error of resting our justification, or the assurance of it, upon such internal effects of faith in the great fact of the redemption, is destructive of that very peace which justification secures. It is not only the fact that our feelings change, and are thus unreliable as evidences of the established relation of the soul to God, which renders the evidence of feeling so precarious. Even if there were no variations in the sense of peace, even if it were felt by all persons and at all times alike, it would be radically wrong to take this effect of the assurance of faith as the proof of the objective reality to which faith clings. The soul is justified not because it feels so, or because it feels the peace which results from the fact that it is sure of being so, but because the Word of God proclaims the fact, and faith apprehends it. The sweet feelings which believers enjoy may, where Satan succeeds in luring the soul to put its trust in them rather than in the promise of God, prove to the unwary an occasion of falling from grace.

The doctrine of Justification by faith finds a strong confirmation in the experience of believers; but never can it be made to rest upon such experience. If a person believes it only upon this ground, he does not believe at all, and all his pretended peace is a mere delusion; for only that is faith which clings to the word and promise of God, be the feelings what they may. God is good, whether we feel good or not; and Christ died for our sins and secured our pardon, whether we rejoice in the hope of glory or not; and the facts as announced in the Gospel we are to believe on the testimony of God. All that experience can do is to add its confirmation to the truth, which, except to our infirmity, needs no confirmation.

111

Our fathers referred frequently to the soothing effect of the Scriptural doctrine of justification upon the believer's soul, as against the disheartening effect of the false doctrine of the Romish Church, which cuts off even the possibility of obtaining the peace which Christ came to bring; but never did they dream of reversing the order, after the manner of fanatics, in which justification by faith and peace with God stand to each other. A doctrine that allows of no peace to the soul must be false. The true doctrine must bring peace. But there may be a false peace, and the only way to secure true peace is to believe the declaration made to us that our sins are forgiven. The peace in our hearts is neither the cause of our justification, nor the cause of our assurance that such justification is ours; the cause of it is the grace of God in Christ, and the cause of our assurance is the divine announcement which faith embraces. But this peace is a blessed effect which grows out of the assurance of faith, and which gives us cheer in the rough journey of life. "Peace I leave with you," our loving Lord declares; "My peace I give unto you; not as the world giveth, give I unto you. Let not your heart be troubled, neither let it be afraid." (John 14:27.) And this peace is ours through faith in His name, who is our peace. There is no peace to those who are without Christ; there is no peace to those who trust in their own possessions or performances, even though they cry peace; there is peace only in the Prince of peace: "being justified by faith, we have peace with God through our Lord Jesus Christ"

Section 2.

IT SECURES SANCTIFICATION.

Nothing has been more frequently urged against the precious doctrine of Justification by faith than this, that it renders sinners carnally secure, instils a false peace, deprives them of all motives for activity in good works, and renders the Church an assembly of careless idlers and dissolute sensualists, who care nothing about holiness because it is not necessary to salvation; and nothing could be more erroneous, or indicate greater ignorance of the doctrine to which the objection is made.

It certainly is true that the sinner is not justified by the deeds of the law; and it is, therefore, true also that the hope of obtaining salvation through the merit of good works cannot, by those who hold the Bible doctrine of justification by faith, be a motive to their performance. If there were no other motive to pursue holiness than this servile one of desiring to render God our debtor, against whom we would have a right to present our claim on the judgment day, it would be true that we who believe in Christ that we might be justified by faith, have no motive to live righteously and godly and soberly in this present world. But that there is no power but selfishness to move us in the way of godliness, that nothing can impel Christians to walk worthy of God but the hope of obtaining wages for their service, only those can maintain who have not yet been blessed with a clear view of the economy of grace and a happy experience of its beneficent provisions.

We might appeal, in answer to the objections made and in proof of the salutary effect of the doctrine in this regard, to the activity and zeal and self-denying labors of the early Church, in which the pure doctrine as the Bible teaches it was universally received and everywhere practically applied; we might point to the work of the individuals and parties who, when the errors of Rome had spread their enervating poison over the greater portion of Christendom, continued in the apostles' doctrine and fellowship and were fervent in spirit, serving the Lord; we might refer to the mighty men of the Reformation, and to the work of the Church in which that Reformation was wrought, the abundant labors and sufferings of three and a half centuries bearing witness before all people to the effect of the doctrine upon the life of believers; and no one could complain of unfairness in the method of argumentation. Let history decide whether these things be so. But we deem it sufficient merely to suggest this line of argument, that the mouths of those who know not what they say may be silenced — millions of witnesses testifying against them. Our object here is rather to explain the doctrine by showing what its effect must be in practical life.

The natural man hates God and His will. If any effort is made to perform His commandments, it is not because the heart is in coincidence with the divine law, but because punishment is dreaded. "They that are after the flesh do mind the things of the flesh; but they that are after the Spirit, the things of the Spirit. For to be carnally minded is death; but to be spiritually minded is life and peace. Because the carnal mind is enmity against God; for it is not subject to the law of God, neither indeed can be." (Rom, 8:5-7.) External conformity is the most that it can accomplish, and this is very imperfect. But external conformity is not fulfillment of the law and is not holiness; the heart remains at enmity with God notwithstanding all endeavors to comply with the requirements of the law. The servile motive furnished by the fear of punishment never can produce true holiness; it can do so just as little in Romanism and other sectarian systems of the present day as it could in Judaism. A motive more effectual is offered where the doctrine of justification by free grace in Christ is apprehended in faith. "For God hath not given us the spirit of fear, but of power and of love and of a sound mind." (2 Tim. 1:7.)

Faith in the atonement made by our Savior makes all things new. God ceases to appear to our souls as an angry tyrant, who gives laws which it is impossible for us to obey, and who punishes all our disobedience. He ceases to be a hateful object, because His love be- comes manifest. Our impulse before was to hide ourselves from His terrible presence, but now is to seek His loving face. His wrath, is averted, and the light of His countenance shines upon us in grace and mercy. He now seems what He really is, the fountain of every blessing and the God of all consolation. All slavish fear is removed, and with the confidence of children we cry, Abba, Father! Christ has purchased us with His own precious blood and rendered full satisfaction to the righteousness of God for us; this we believe, and in this we are glad. In the strength of this faith we now offer our service with a free and cheerful heart, loving God because He first loved us. "Blessing, and honor, and glory, and power, be unto Him that sitteth upon the throne, and unto the Lamb for ever and ever."

Not the hope of meriting life and wresting, as it were, a crown of glory from the unwilling hands of Jehovah, but gratitude for grace and every blessing mercifully bestowed upon us in measures beyond all we could ask or think, is the motive which prompts us to praise His glorious name, with all our powers, in word and work. This, too, is the powerful motive which the Gospel presents. It does not tell us to work that God may be gracious to us; but to be in labors abundant because He has been gracious to us and is gracious now. "As ye have therefore received Christ Jesus the Lord, so walk ye in Him: rooted and built up in Him, and established in the faith, as ye have been taught, abounding therein with thanksgiving." (Col. 2:6, 7.) Christians are an active people in all holiness, because the love of Christ constraineth them. "For we are His workmanship, created in Christ Jesus unto good works, which God hath before ordained that we should walk in them." (Eph. 2:10.) Those are to be pitied who can find in this no motive to an energetic prosecution of the work of the Lord, and no power for consecration to His blessed service; who can conceive of no effort to do His pleasure except by coercion; who can think of no other effect produced by the believing recognition of Jesus' work and passion for the salvation of our souls, than that we become idlers who despise His gracious will and treat His love with scorn. Let them but come to Jesus and see! This would give them a better conception of the nature and power of that faith which clings to the dear Redeemer and finds every joy in Him.

Luther, who apprehended and taught the doctrine of Justification by faith alone, without the deeds of the law, with a clearness and a power that has never been equaled since, says with reference to this point: "Faith is not the human fancy and dream which some call faith. When they perceive that people may hear and say much about faith, and still it is not followed by amendment of life and good works, they erroneously conclude that faith is not sufficient, but that good works are also necessary to justification and salvation. The reason of this is, that, when they hear the Gospel, they, by their own power, form an opinion which they express in the words 'I believe,' and this they hold to be true faith. But as this is a human notion and figment which the heart never experiences, it accomplishes nothing and is followed by no amendment. Faith, however, is a divine work in us which changes the heart and through which we are born of God. (John 1:13.) It destroys the old Adam, makes us new creatures in heart, soul, sense, and all our powers, and brings with it the Holy Spirit. Oh, faith is a living, busy, active, mighty power; it is impossible for it not to be incessantly doing good. Nor does it ask whether good works must be done: before the question is asked it has done them, and is perpetually doing them. He who does not perform such works has no faith, who stumbles about in quest of faith and good works, but knows not what faith is nor what good works are, much as he prates and prattles about them. Faith is a living, inflexible trust in the grace of God, so certain that it would face a thousand deaths. And this knowledge of divine grace and confidence in it renders us joyous, and bold, and cheerful towards God and all creatures, which is the work of the Holy Ghost by faith. Hence man becomes willing and eager to do good to every person, to serve every one, to suffer everything, for the pleasure and glory of God, who has given him such grace. Thus it is as impossible to separate works from faith as to separate light and heat in flames. Therefore beware of your own erring thoughts, and of vain babblers, who profess to be wise in judging of faith and works, but who are the greatest fools. Pray God that He may work faith in you; otherwise you will forever remain without faith, do and fancy what you may."

True, living faith in the redemption, which appropriates the full merits of Christ and gives the soul joy and peace, sanctifies the soul, as it never can be sanctified under any system that rejects justification by faith.

Section 3.

IT RENDERS GLORY TO GOD.

No doctrine of Justification that has ever been taught so completely and so exclusively gives the glory of man's salvation to God as that which forms the great material principle of the Reformation. All others ascribe some merit and some praise to men; and in proportion as they glorify the creature do they detract from the glory of the Savior, without whom we can do nothing. "Where is boasting then? It is excluded. By what law? of works? Nay, but by the law of faith." (Rom. 3:27.)

The end of man's creation and preservation, of his redemption and sanctification, is the glory of the Creator and Redeemer. For this all things were made. "Thou art worthy, O Lord, to receive glory and honor and power; for Thou hast created all things, and for Thy pleasure they are and were created." (Rev. 4:11.) Any doctrine that derogates from this glory which belongs to Him, or would divide it with the sinful creature, must on that account be false. The whole work of grace necessarily tends to His glory. "Glory to God in the highest" was the song of the angels when Jesus was born; and the Church of the Redeemer never ceases to say: "Now unto Him that is able to do exceeding abundantly above all that we ask or think, according to the power that worketh in us, unto Him be glory in the Church by Christ Jesus throughout all ages, world without end. Amen."

Justification brings peace to the soul. But this peace does not exalt the individual who possesses it. He cannot have it without clinging to Jesus as its only ground and cause. But faith in the Savior as its source is incompatible with that proud self-complacency which bases all upon personal exertions and merits. He is our peace. There can be no justification without recognizing this, and where this is recognized there, can be no ascription of honor to self as though peace were a product of nature and not of grace.

Justification renders us active in good works. But these works of the law contribute nothing to justification and secure for us no merit. They do not exist before the faith which appropriates the righteousness of Christ, and have nothing to do with this appropriation, of which they are effects, — in no sense grounds or causes. The works are necessary; but their necessity is not that of aids to justification. The glory of all our works, as well as the glory of all from which these works proceed, belongs to God alone, and is seen by the justified person to belong to God alone. As he ascribes all the praise of his justification to the Lord our Righteousness, so he performs all his works for His glory, according to the divine will as expressed by St. Paul: "Whether therefore ye eat or drink, or whatsoever ye do, do all to the glory of God," (1 Cor. 10:31,) and, "Whatsoever ye do, in word or deed, do all in the name of the Lord Jesus, giving thanks to God and the Father by Him." (Col. 3:17.) True faith, which apprehends the forgiveness of sins as offered freely through the means of grace, renders the believer active in the work of the Lord, that God may be glorified by his life and labors, and prompts him, at the same time, to give God all the glory, because to Him all is seen to be due.

Justification insures salvation; for where there is forgiveness sins there of course is also life and salvation. But as justification is wholly an act of God's grace for Christ's sake, there can be glory ascribed to no other than to Him. For they have fallen from grace who would be justified and saved by the deeds of the law: Christ is become of no effect to them. Salvation is found in Jesus only. Those who seek it elsewhere, so as to give the praise to another, never find it. Those who find it in Jesus are grateful, and give the glory to Him alone.

What is recorded of the father of the faithful is applicable, though it be not in the same degree, to all believers: "He staggered not at the promise of God through unbelief; but was strong in the faith, giving glory to God." (Rom. 4:20.) The Reformers declare, in the Apology of the Augsburg Confession, and repeat the saying in various forms at other places: "The honor which is due to Christ we must not give to the law or to our miserable works." The true believer has no desire to do this. Any doctrine which teaches him to do it is condemned by this very fact, and all who are jealous for the honor of their blessed Lord should unite in denouncing it and warning against it. "God forbid that I should glory, save in the cross of our Lord Jesus Christ." (Gal. 6:14.)

The pure doctrine of justification makes the soul humble; for we are conscious of deserving nothing but condemnation, and of having all by the grace of God through Jesus Christ. But while we decrease, Christ increases. It humbles us to exalt our Savior. It gives constant joy and peace, and supplies the motive, in gratitude, to consecrate our all to Him. "Thanks be to God, who giveth us the victory through our Lord Jesus Christ. Therefore, my beloved brethren, be ye steadfast, immovable, always abounding in the work of the Lord, forasmuch as ye know that your labor is not in vain in the Lord." (2 Cor. 15:57, 58.) Those who hold and experience, the truth of the precious doctrine never weary in His praise. They live not unto themselves, but unto Him who died for us and rose again, "that God in all things may be glorified through Jesus Christ, to whom be praise and dominion forever and ever. Amen." (1 Peter 4:11.)

CONCLUSION.

THE doctrine which has been set forth is precious is beyond the powers of language to describe. It is the great central truth of Christianity, which is the only true religion, and which manifests itself as such by giving "knowledge of salvation unto His people by the remission of their sins, through the tender mercy of our God, whereby the dayspring from on high hath visited us, to give light to them that sit in darkness and in the shadow of death, to guide our feet into the way of peace." (Luke 1:77-79.) It is the glory of the Evangelical Lutheran Church, whose single aim always was and is and shall be to honor her Lord and save the souls purchased by His own dear blood.

Nor should we flatter ourselves that the energy and zeal with which the Church proclaimed this cardinal doctrine in the days of the Reformation are needless now, when Protestantism has gained so firm a foothold in the world and is cherished by so many millions of enlightened people. It is the article against which the great foe of human happiness directs his craft and power as persistently as ever. The truth shall stand, in spite of every effort that is made to overthrow it. The foundation of God standeth sure; the word of the Lord abideth forever. But many are misled, and while the doctrine stands, and must stand, many have fallen and many are in daily peril of falling. Therefore, the love of Christ and of the souls which He has redeemed should constrain us to study it and teach it unweariedly, that what lies in our power may be done to extend the peace and comfort and everlasting salvation which it brings, and preserve it to men until the latest generations.

Of such efforts there is all the more need, because many who claim to be children of the Reformation have either abandoned it or permitted its glory to become dim. It is at once a pleasant and a painful task to declare that the Evangelical Lutheran Church alone retains it in its purity and power. We record it with joyous gratitude to God, that He has preserved the blessed light of the Gospel in our Lutheran Church, so that, through her teaching and confessing, men may learn with certainty the way of salvation and find peace unto their souls. But we perceive with grief that doctrines are taught in other churches which conflict, with the simple evangelical plan of salvation

119

through faith in Christ alone, and which render it more or less difficult to find the way to heaven. Not only does the Romish Church continue her wicked warfare against the Gospel, but the Romish leaven has pervaded Protestant denominations, to a greater or less extent, all around us. When it is taught, for instance, that the sin innate in man is not sin, or does not subject to condemnation; that the redemption is accomplished for only an elect: portion of our race; that faith avails for our salvation only by being active in good works; that the word of absolution becomes effectual only through man's repentance or amendment; that Baptism and the Lord's Supper cannot convey remission of sin, but that this is dependent upon a certain degree of holiness attained; that man must seek peace in his sanctification; that perfect holiness is attainable on earth, and that only those who have attained it have the full comfort of the Gospel; that no one can be certain of the truth revealed unto salvation in the Scriptures; that our pious feelings are the criteria of our adoption as God's children; when such and similar opinions are taught as the Gospel of Christ, the influence of Romanism, with its anti-evangelical spirit, is plain to every eye which the grace of God has enabled to see clearly. There is no doctrine whose renewed study is more needful now than that of Justification by faith alone. Our dear Redeemer, grant that its power may become more manifest in the consecrated lives and the triumphant deaths of Christian people!

O Christ, Thou Lamb of God that takest away the sins of the world, grant us Thy peace.

Made in United States
Troutdale, OR
09/24/2024

23100722R00076